LEFT WITHOUT A TRACE

Understanding what truly matters in life and discovering the purpose that drives your existence.

NAMAKAU PAULA S. BRISCOE

DEDICATION

My deepest gratitude goes to God the Father, my Creator, and the Lover of my soul. Without Him, my writing would not be possible, and for that, I owe Him everything. My deep relationship with Him has been my greatest comfort during the darkest seasons of my life.

I dedicate this book to the most precious woman in my life, who brought me into this world as the vessel through which I was delivered. She has imparted an abundance of wisdom, knowledge, and understanding that have shaped the life I now live. To my incredible mother, Naluca Brigid Mwikisa- Simbotwe, you forever reside in the deepest recesses of my heart, and your spirit resonated with me throughout the writing process of this book.

I also dedicate this accomplishment to my beloved daughter, Sepo Briscoe, who has taught me to access a reservoir of strength I never knew existed within me. Sepo, your love will endure eternally, and your spirit will forever dwell within my heart, thoughts, and life. I eagerly anticipate the day when we will be reunited with your Kuku (Grandma) Naluca in heaven.

CONTENTS

FOREWORD

In the vast expanse of existence, humanity is confronted with fundamental questions about the purpose of our being and the significance of our presence in this world. We journey through life, seeking answers, discovering meaning, and striving for fulfilment. It is within this intricate tapestry of human experiences that *Left Without a Trace* finds its place.

In this deeply personal and poignant memoir, the author invites us into the depths of her grief and the profound impact of loss on her life. With raw honesty and heartfelt emotion, she recounts the painful experiences of bidding farewell to her loved ones and the enduring sorrow that accompanies such farewells. The author's journey begins with the heart- wrenching loss of her own mother. She vividly recalls the somber act of witnessing her being laid to rest, etching the scene in her memory as she turned away, leaving her body in the embrace of the earth. The anguish and devastation of that moment shaped her understanding of the fragility of life, leaving indelible marks on her soul.

The journey back to her homeland, Zambia, becomes a painful pilgrimage to bid farewell to her mother and best friend. The author shares the anguish and turmoil she experienced during the long flight, questioning God, and grappling with the unfairness of her mother's untimely departure. In the midst of her grief, she receives a profound revelation that brings comfort and reassurance, reminding her that their mother is at peace in a beautiful place.

As the author navigates unfamiliar territories and grapples with the unimaginable pain of grief, she comes to realize that her life had been different and, in many ways, better because of her mother's presence. Her mother's influence instilled in her values of common sense and wisdom, emphasizing the importance of using one's judgement in various life situations. The author reflects on the cherished memories of her mother and expresses profound gratitude for the woman who shaped her into the person she is today.

As you embark on this literary voyage, you will traverse the realms of reflection, introspection, and the pursuit of freedom. The chapters within this book paint a vivid picture of the human condition, capturing the essence of our hopes and dreams and the challenges that shape our lives. Through poignant stories and heartfelt observations, the author invites us to contemplate the choices we make, the paths we follow, and the profound impact they have on our existence.

Left Without a Trace serves as a beacon of hope amidst the trials and tribulations of life. It offers solace, encouragement, and a gentle nudge to ponder the deeper questions that lie within each of us. As you navigate through its pages, allow yourself to immerse in the stories, contemplate their meaning, and to glean wisdom from the shared experiences.

May this book ignite a flame within your heart—a flame that inspires you to embrace the open windows of opportunity, to seize the present moment, and to cultivate a life that embodies freedom, resilience, and unwavering hope. May you be reminded that even in the face of uncertainty, you possess the power to leave a trace—a trace of love, of purpose, and of the indomitable spirit that defines the human experience.

Cathy Rivers
Renowned Editor.

CHAPTER 1

PATHWAY TO FREEDOM

How do you feel when you wake up and the first thing you see, as you draw the curtain, is the bright blue sky with the sun radiating its rays directly at you? It's so vibrant and full of promise, signalling the start of a wonderful new day. That sunshine is always a delightful way to begin each day, filling you with excitement and amazement. The sight of that beautiful blue sky, especially after a gloomy day, uplifts your heart and brings a smile to your face.

In the Bible, it is said, 'Light is sweet, and it pleases the eye to see the sun.' It triggers a surge of feel-good hormones within you, igniting hope and joy as you anticipate the goodness the day holds. In my neighbourhood, I often wake up to the sounds of seagulls engaging in their natural communication, gracefully flying from one rooftop to another.

I find my greatest strength in the serene and still moments of the morning. It often takes me a while to leave the comfort of my bed, as I observe the unfolding scenes of life through my bedroom window.

During these moments, I dedicate a few precious minutes to silent meditation and expressions of gratitude. I reflect upon the abundant blessings bestowed upon me by God and embrace the fresh opportunity granted to me as I embark on another day of living.

I am deeply appreciative of life and the invaluable freedom that accompanies this precious gift. It is a privilege that should never be taken for granted or misused by those who are alive. I am often in awe of the boundless liberty enjoyed by birds. Unlike human beings, they possess an even greater degree of entitlement to soar through the sky, alight wherever they please, and nourish themselves from any person's garden as often as they desire, without needing permission or encountering restrictions.

One morning, I woke up to yet another brilliant blue sky. As I gazed out of my window, my attention was captured by a moth fluttering about near the glass. I became somewhat fixated on this intriguing sight, particularly because the moth appeared larger than usual.

Curiosity piqued; I focused my attention on studying this flying creature as it flapped its wings behind the net curtain. I pondered whether it was inside or outside my window. Upon closer observation, I discovered that it was actually inside my bedroom, trapped behind the net curtain.

At that moment, I became intensely interested in witnessing its escape. The moth seemed disoriented, fluttering aimlessly within the confinements of the net curtain, desperately trying to find a way out. It became clear to me that its lack of direction was keeping it trapped. I felt an overwhelming urge to assist it in finding its path to freedom.

So, despite knowing that my older son had a deep fear of flying creatures, I called out to him, hoping he would muster the courage to assist in guiding the trapped moth towards an open window. I wanted to give it a try and see just how brave my son could be in rescuing the helpless creature.

Despite his initial reluctance, my son summoned the courage to open one of the windows, hoping to provide the trapped moth with a pathway to freedom. However, I noticed that even with the window open, the moth seemed unaware of the opportunity to escape. Instead, it remained in its confined space, flying towards the open window and then returning to its familiar spot. I expected it to sense the gentle breeze wafting through the open window and swiftly make its way out.

Eventually, I found myself perplexed as to why the moth couldn't recognize the window as its means of escape, persistently flapping its wings in a struggle to break free. It was at this point that I decided to call upon my younger daughter, who held a lesser fear of flying insects, to come and assist in rescuing the moth from its pitiful plight.

As my daughter attempted to guide the moth by lifting the net curtain and pointing it towards the open window, to my surprise, the moth flew in the opposite direction. It seemed strangely drawn to flying around the closed window instead of heading towards the open window for its escape. Despite our persistent efforts to encourage it towards the open window, the moth stubbornly clung to the closed area of the window, refusing to take the obvious pathway to freedom.

Frustration grew within us, and my daughter eventually released the curtain, allowing the moth to find its own way out. I gazed at the moth, even attempting to communicate verbally with the helpless creature, urging it to recognize that the window was open for its release. However, no matter how much I spoke to it, the moth continued to struggle in the same area around the closed window, seemingly oblivious to the freedom just within its reach.

I, too, found myself running out of options and simply lay in bed, continuing to observe the moth, hoping that it would eventually comprehend our offer of freedom.

Regrettably, I reached a point of resignation, realizing that every intervention I had made failed to yield results. Much to my frustration, I reluctantly shifted my gaze away from it, as all my attempts to assist had proven fruitless. After some time had passed, I glanced over to see if I could locate the moth, only to discover that it was no longer there.

I remain uncertain whether it successfully escaped or perhaps perished in its relentless pursuit of freedom. I never found any remnants of the moth, so I can only assume that it may have indeed exited through the open window.

It was during that observation of the moth that a moment of realization hit me, illuminating the striking resemblance between the life of a human being and that of that moth. How so, you may wonder? What I had just witnessed mirrored the experience of individuals who find themselves trapped behind a metaphorical curtain, unable to perceive an open window leading to freedom.

At times, people fail to seize the moments and opportunities that present themselves. Despite open windows of opportunity, humans may persist in fruitless efforts to find alternative escape routes. Some opportunities are fleeting, and when we miss them, it is often due to our failure to recognize the assistance being offered to us. The helping hand that lifts the curtain, making it easier to grasp an opportunity, often goes unappreciated as we prefer to remain within our comfort zones.

Although the windows of opportunity may open, we, like the struggling moth, fail to see them as pathways to freedom. Instead, we choose to remain in familiar territories, even if they entail a life of suffering and mediocrity. Perhaps we find solace in the familiar or harbour distrust towards those who extend a helping hand. Consequently, we settle for less than the best, denying ourselves the opportunity to reach our fullest potential.

The story of the moth carries a valuable lesson. Initially, the moth struggled to escape, encountering closed windows at every turn. However, when a helper appeared, willing to lift the curtain and offer it freedom, the moth hesitated to trust the genuine nature of the opportunity. It may have perceived the helper as a potential threat to its well-being.

Similarly, humans often fail to recognize the open windows of opportunity that are accessible to them. We may be skeptical of the authenticity of the opportunities that arise and choose to remain within the confines of our comfort zones.

Despite our earnest efforts to assist the moth in finding a safe exit, it did not cooperate. Its ultimate fate and whereabouts remain a mystery. It seemingly vanished without a trace, existing solely within the confines of my memory.

Unfortunately, many of us humans find ourselves living like that trapped moth, ultimately ending up in despair and hardship by not seizing the opportunities presented to us. Perhaps due to past experiences or trust issues, we tend to generalize and assume that all people are the same, which leads us to struggle alone instead of reaching out for help.

However, it is often outside our comfort zones where the best things in life await. Similar to the moth, we may fail to realize that there are individuals who genuinely have our best interests at heart and are advocating for our well-being. Instead, we choose to remain in what we perceive as a safe place, even if it hinders our growth and potential.

Nature has an abundance of lessons to teach us, and the story of the moth is just a small part of the vast reservoir of wisdom found in living creatures and plants. By paying close attention to nature, we can gain valuable insights and learn important life lessons.

CHAPTER 2

HERE TODAY, GONE TOMORROW

I continue with my account of life, shifting towards a sombre and weighty tone as I grapple with the realization of the unpredictable nature of the world we inhabit. Numerous thoughts occupy my mind, confronting me with a stark reality that lingers each day I exist. Thoughts such as the unsettling notion that today could be my last day on Earth startle me, causing a chill to run down my spine. Much like the moth, I may find myself desperately seeking an escape from a dire situation, only to discover that reaching the open window is an elusive accomplishment.

Although, in a peculiar sort of way, these thoughts push me to do the best that I can with the gift of life given today. I can only imagine your perspective as you read this opening chapter. It is quite possible that this topic is not one you may wish to encounter or delve into, and I completely understand.

Perhaps, like me, you have an aversion to sorrowful tales and find yourself avoiding the news due to its often-pervasive atmosphere of despair and negativity. Bad news resembles an interminable narrative of sorrow, devoid of hope, and consistently evokes sighs of sadness and a sense of despair whenever it reaches my ears.

It is possible that, like me, you reside in a realm of impossibilities, embracing dreams with the unwavering belief that one day they will materialize on life's stage. Perhaps you envision yourself achieving remarkable accomplishments, traversing various corners of the globe, and basking in a life that resonates with your passions.

It is likely that you possess a vivid imagination, dear to your heart, that you yearn to manifest, leading you to envision a long, contented, serene, and gratifying existence.

The dread of death, loss, sickness, disability, limitation, poverty, and disease is an enemy that robs you of time and cheats you out of living a complete and satisfactory life. I am gradually coming to understand that poverty, disease, and the loss of loved ones are some of humanity's greatest foes.

Even the mere mention of death or dying is often regarded as a taboo subject by many individuals. Such topics are often avoided and swiftly brushed aside, kept at a safe distance.

There are many among us who yearn to embrace the present reality of our dreams, knowing that they have the potential to manifest. We hold great hopes for tomorrow, as it offers a fresh start and a new array of opportunities.

In the midst of dark circumstances that often plague humanity, tomorrow carries the promise of a new dawn, a glimmer of light that shines through. However, none of us is exempt from the pain and despair that afflicts the human experience.

The unpredictability of life never ceases to amaze me. As I grow older, I gain a deeper understanding of the importance of utilizing my time wisely and not taking it for granted. I strive to cherish each moment, season, and period in my life, and I make a conscious effort not to take people for granted.

Moreover, the realization that nothing in this world is guaranteed keeps me focused on fulfilling the necessary tasks and responsibilities at hand. What we possess today may be lost tomorrow, urging us to embrace a sense of urgency and appreciation for the present.

Hopefully, my life's story will serve as a beacon of hope, a source of strength, evoking both tears and moments of joy. It will portray the reality of finding peace and resilience amidst affliction and adversity. You may question and wonder, "How can I continue to dream and hold onto hope in a world that feels so uncertain?" The answer is simple, you can still dream as long as you have life within you.

Even in the midst of sorrow, or while lying in a hospital bed, facing a daunting diagnosis beyond your control, you can still dream. This is because hope is a guaranteed promise for those who believe in God. If you're anything like me, you might find solace in a beautiful love story with a delightful happy ending.

I used to adore fairy tales, and while I still appreciate them, as I grow older, my perspective has changed with the realization that my inner strength comes more from my faith in God rather than from the fairy tales that always conclude with the phrase, "and they lived happily ever after."

Sadly, not all stories conclude with a "happily ever after" ending. However, it is important to acknowledge that in many instances, we have the power to shape our own happy endings by making wise choices in life. Nevertheless, there are occasions when despite our best efforts, we come to realize that we do not have complete control over everything, and that life offers no guarantees.

In such moments, we continue to pursue a path of goodness and righteousness, even in the face of uncertainty, and hold on to hope for the best possible outcomes. It is important to recognize that there are often circumstances beyond our control; life can unfold in unexpected ways for all individuals.

In moments of deep contemplation, I often find myself trembling at the thought of unfulfilled dreams and unrealized visions. The greatest tragedy in life, in my opinion, is to depart from this world with untapped potential and without achieving the purpose for which one was created. The idea of living a life that leaves no trace of ever having existed fills me with profound trepidation.

What words could I possibly utter when I stand face to face with my Creator, knowing that I have nothing to show for the gifts and opportunities bestowed upon me? A mere gravestone with my name, birth date, and date of death, separated by a simple dash, representing my time on Earth. It symbolizes a life that may or may not have made a significant impact on others. For me, this is far from satisfactory.

I yearn to leave a legacy, to touch lives, and to fulfil the mandate that has been entrusted to me. I believe that when we are born, we come endowed with so much treasure within us. So, at our final hour, we need to leave the Earth empty, knowing that we have deposited all we have in adding value to the lives of others. Living life with a definite purpose and a clear objective in mind should be each person's delight.

However, the events and circumstances of our lives sometimes fail to accurately depict our true purpose on Earth, both in life and in death. I once heard someone say that the richest places on Earth are not the gold mines of the world, but the cemeteries where many find their final resting place.

Recently, while listening to an interview, I came across Colonel Harland Sanders, the founder of Kentucky Fried Chicken (KFC), who discovered his passion for cooking at age 9, and later founded his famous brand at the age of 62.

Colonel Sanders wisely remarked, "There is no point in being the wealthiest person in the cemetery because you cannot conduct any business there." This statement resonates with this truth; In the race of life, all runners ultimately start from birth and end at the same place in death. Therefore, it matters greatly what you do with what you have been given. This has prompted me to ponder the following questions: How many individuals have passed away without ever truly experiencing a full life? How many of them possessed remarkable ideas and inventions that were never brought to fruition? How many departed with captivating stories that will never be read by anyone? And what about the artists who had incredible songs that could have topped the music charts but were never sung?

It is disheartening to acknowledge that numerous people have departed from this world without leaving a trace, yet they carried within them hidden treasures and dreams that remained unrealized.

Sadly, many gifts and talents have been laid to rest, never to be witnessed, heard, or experienced by the living. The contemplation of these realities sends a chill down my spine each time I encounter the countless gravestones adorning the cemetery.

The cemetery conceals numerous enigmatic mysteries and untold tales of buried treasures that will forever remain undiscovered or unknown. As I contemplate the gravestones, I am drawn to the comparison and contrasting effect of birth and death dates, representing one's entry and exit from this world. It is disheartening to witness the stark contrast in the length of lives, with some tragically cut short compared to others.

Each individual is uniquely positioned on this Earth, endowed with their own distinct gifts and purpose. I often find myself wondering about the person behind the inscription and pondering the potential they held, the destiny they were meant to fulfil, and whether they were able to carry out their intended mission in life.

I keenly observe the diverse styles and designs of the gravestones, the architectural elements surrounding the graves, the presence of family members buried in the same plot, and even the presence or absence of flowers adorning the graves.

These observations serve as distressing reminders of the fleeting nature of life and its inherent fragility. They prompt me to acknowledge the unpredictable nature of my existence and the uncertainty of when my own turn will come to join the countless individuals lying in the cemetery. I understand that thoughts and conversations concerning mortality can be discomforting and often avoided by many.

However, as much as I love 'the happily ever after endings', death remains an undeniable reality of our human existence. It is an inherent part of the cycle of life, where there is a time for both birth and death. Death is an inescapable aspect of our journey, a universal certainty that eventually awaits every human being.

Though it may sound sombre, there is solace in recognizing that the death of the physical body does not mark the ultimate end, but rather the conclusion of one's earthly life.

For those who believe in God, there is the assurance of heaven—an eternal realm. The remarkable aspect of death is that we have the opportunity to spend eternity with Jesus Christ, thus finding comfort, peace, and hope in this understanding.

CHAPTER 3

MY MOTHER

I have witnessed, with profound pain, sorrow, and horror, the sombre act of loved ones being lowered into the ground, as their final resting place. I still remember, in disbelief, the moment when my own mother was laid to rest, etching the scene in my memory as we turned away, leaving her body in the embrace of the earth. The anguish of my heart and deep sorrow intensified as I faced the heart-wrenching reality of my own child being laid to rest in the ground too.

Those final moments of bidding farewell have been, without a doubt, the most agonizing experiences I have endured as a human being. The pain, anguish, and devastation of those farewells have left indelible marks on my soul, shaping my understanding of the fragility of life.

The journey of life has taken me to several unfamiliar territories. Never have I known such pain, nor been tested beyond what I thought I could not bear in my human body. The misery that wraps itself with a nametag called 'loss' is agonizing beyond words. In the face of such tragedies, attempting to find meaning or make sense of it all becomes an exercise in futility.

When grief strikes close to home, the pain and confusion become unimaginable, enveloping one's being with an overwhelming sense of anguish and disorientation. The unsettling reality is that this cycle does not come to an end, but instead continues with more unforeseen deaths in the future. I have observed and heard through the news of celebrities' passing away, and witnessed the profound grief experienced by their loved ones. Regardless of one's societal status or role, death is an inescapable certainty that befalls every one of us, and the pain felt in its wake is undeniably real, irrespective of one's identity or position.

I could easily fill the pages of a book with countless cherished memories of my mother. In the brief time that she graced my life, I can confidently state that the woman I have become today is a genuine reflection of the values she imparted to me during my formative years.

I am forever indebted to my mother, Naluca Brigid Mwikisa-Simbotwe, and I wholeheartedly honour her with profound gratitude.

Expressing how much I miss her would be an understatement; she was not only my world but also the first love of my life. However, I am eternally grateful for the time I had with her, albeit only 24 short years as my earthly and biological mother. Her existence held a purpose, and her profound influence on my life has left an indelible mark that will endure for eternity.

Through my mother, I received valuable home training and character-building lessons. Her discipline and advice shaped me during my younger years, and I am truly grateful to God for blessing me with such an amazing woman to call 'Ima' which means Mum. While she wasn't perfect, in my eyes and in every way, she was imperfectly perfect. She was God's chosen vessel who brought me into this world, and she was perfect for me.

My mother was a beautiful, hardworking, determined, and optimistic woman. She had achieved several of her goals and desires at a young age, something that many women her age had not accomplished. Even as a young widow, she tirelessly worked hard to provide her children with a good and stable upbringing. She devoted herself to giving us a high-quality life and exposing us to the world.

I remember how my childhood was filled with as few obstacles as possible. As a child, I had a lot of fun growing up, but like most children, I took the good times for granted, assuming they would last forever. Nobody really prepared me for the inevitable hardships and sorrows of life.

Although my mother taught me many things about life, she did not teach me how to navigate through life without her. Mum always shielded us from pain and difficulties when my siblings and me were young. Even during the occasional dull moments, my life felt like an endless party of playing, laughing, visiting family members, and going on holidays, both to my grandmother in the village and even abroad.

From a young age, my siblings and me had the opportunity to travel to various destinations around the world and interact with people from different nationalities. I still vividly remember my first flying experience when I was around 8 years old. Our usual destination was to visit my grandmother, who resided in the village of Western Province of Zambia, the country of my birth. I didn't mind flying to see her because the alternative of travelling by car was not appealing to me. The road journey would take hours due to the poor road conditions at that time, which is not too exciting when you are a child.

From an early age, I have distinct memories of my mother instructing my siblings and me on table manners and etiquette. I often felt awkward and pressured by the expectations placed upon us. I couldn't comprehend why a meal had to be accompanied by such a formal atmosphere. All I wanted was to enjoy my food using my fingers, as I was accustomed to doing.

However, we were taught how to set the table properly, arranging different types of cutleries and placing glasses on specific sides. It felt as though we were dining at a Michelin-starred restaurant because my mother had a perfectionist personality.

Looking back, I realize that my mother was sharing with us everything she had learned during her many travels, making us her students at home. The emphasis on culinary excellence and the use of fork and knife were foreign customs to us, as they were not commonly used in Zambian culture; we typically ate our traditional Zambian staple foods with our fingers, which I found enjoyable and effortless.

However, on certain days when my mother prepared what seemed like a different and foreign cuisine, she would insist that we use cutlery and dine at the table. We were taught proper etiquette and table manners, and it often felt like we were constantly under scrutiny, as if a camera were watching our every move. My mother was strict when it came to following these protocols and closely monitored our behaviour. We were expected to always exhibit our best behaviour. In addition, there were specific rules to abide by, such as no loud chewing, no resting elbows on the table, no gulping water from the glass, only sipping was allowed, and no talking with our mouths full, among others. As a young child, I could not comprehend the purpose of all these rules and found the whole affair rather pointless. All I wanted was to enjoy my meal without having to worry about how I handled or chewed my food.

Even though it seemed like a burden at the time, my mother would frequently mention that she was teaching us how to conduct ourselves when dining with important individuals. I would often ponder over her words, wondering when such a situation would arise and how our table manners could possibly relate to meeting notable people.

However, her voice still resonates in my mind, insisting that one day we would share meals with dignitaries, and it was crucial to behave appropriately. As time went on, I came to understand the wisdom behind her teachings. Back then, I failed to grasp the true significance of that training, but now I realize what a rare privilege it was to receive such guidance. Furthermore, our upbringing encompassed learning how to maintain a tidy environment, kitchen duties, and prioritize personal hygiene. Dressing modestly was also emphasized, as etiquette seemed to guide every aspect of our lives and culture, including demonstrating respect for the elderly, valuing God, and education.

As previously mentioned, my siblings and I began travelling to other countries at a time when most of our friends and relatives had never experienced flying before. This was a unique advantage we had because our mother worked for the national airline. Consequently, due to the nature of her profession, we had the privilege of flying on local and international flights from a young age, interacting with people from diverse ethnic backgrounds, and immersing ourselves in different cultures, which facilitated our continuous learning and growth.

When I was around 10 years of age, during one of our trips while transiting in Nairobi, Kenya, our training was put to the test. My mother observed closely to see how we would handle our cutlery and conduct ourselves in a restaurant. It was the first time I truly understood the value of our home training. This experience provided us with a remarkable opportunity to dine in a foreign setting, bringing to life everything we had been taught. The moment of truth had arrived, and I am pleased to say that we all passed the test, earning my mother's approval and pride.

Even though I may not have fully understood or appreciated the home training while it was being given, that particular experience made me truly grateful for the lessons my mother imparted to us. The seemingly unnecessary fuss was actually about creating awareness and providing us with exposure, as she was determined to prepare us for the challenges and realities of the outside world. Looking back, I am eternally thankful for her unwavering efforts.

As mentioned earlier, I can vividly recall the times when my mother would mention the importance of learning to dine with dignitaries or refer to significant individuals in life. At the time, I failed to see the relevance of her words or the impact they would have on our future.

I could not imagine at such a young age who these important people were that my mother spoke about. But now, as I reflect on it, everything makes sense, and I am incredibly grateful for my upbringing and the home training I received. I now pass on those valuable lessons to my own children. Back then, I did not fully realize that my mother held us to a high standard and that we were different from other children.

Despite not having a father figure in our home, my mother made sure that we lacked nothing. While it would have been a different and perhaps positive experience to have known the love of a father, I honestly cannot miss something that I never had, but I distinctly remember my mother saying that life would probably be better if my father were around.

I still find it difficult to imagine the presence of my father because he passed away when I was only 9 months old, leaving me with no memories of him. My mother would often recount how much I was a replica of him. Mum faced many hardships after my father's death, particularly due to the hostility and cruelty from my father's family.

During that time, there were no laws in place to protect widows and orphans from the actions of greedy relatives who would claim ownership of possessions and property, asserting that everything my father had owned now belonged to them, including any assets acquired during his lifetime. In such circumstances, widows were subjected to disrespect, disdain, and dehumanization. They were left with nothing, as everything they and their husbands had worked hard for was taken away by those who had once dined with them and smiled at them while their husbands were alive.

The treatment of widows in such a wicked and inhumane manner was undoubtedly unjust and deeply painful for my mother. It was an experience filled with bitterness and unfairness.

Despite the challenges she faced, my mother embraced the role of being both a mother and a father to her children as a single parent. I am convinced that God showered His grace upon her by providing her with a good job that allowed her to cater for the needs of her family.

Many times, she would remind me that God was by her side. I firmly believe that God indeed watches over those who are in need, including widows, orphans, and fatherless children, as He has promised to care for them.

God truly bestowed uncommon favour upon my mother, and as a result, her enemies were left astonished and humiliated. Throughout my mother's life, I witnessed first-hand how God faithfully provided for us. I can honestly say that I never experienced poverty as a child because all my needs were consistently and adequately met. I cannot even fathom what it means to go to bed hungry because we always had an abundance, often with enough to share generously with others.

CHAPTER 4

CRUSHED BUT NOT BROKEN

Rather unexpectedly, tragedy struck when my mother passed away, entering into eternity. It became evident to me that my life had been different and, in many ways, better than those who had the presence of both parents. This realization stems from the fact that God's hand was always upon my mother, and she received favour both from Him and from others. Reflecting on my life and the privileges my siblings and I enjoyed during our childhood, I now understand that my mother's efforts instilled in me the values of common sense and wisdom. She possessed an abundance of both and consistently emphasized the importance of using our common sense in various life situations. It was one of her favourite expressions, particularly when she wanted to guide or discipline us.

I vividly remember the day when my mother passed away. I can still recall the exact location I was in, the people I was with, and the precise moment when I received the devastating news.

It struck me as peculiar because the person who informed me of her death was not someone close to either me or my mother. It felt as though this relative delivered the news out of spite, without consulting other older members of the family, almost as if her intention was to shatter and crush me.

Nevertheless, the shock of the news overwhelmed me. I wasn't provided with any specific details regarding the circumstances of my mother's passing; all I knew was that she was no longer with us. The impact of this revelation was immediate. I let out a horrified scream upon hearing the news, which was followed by a state of shock and then a profound sense of disbelief that gradually settled in.

As I tried to process the situation, memories of my mother's final visit to England resurfaced. I was residing there at the time, and our time together had been filled with joyous moments of shopping and heartfelt conversations.

During that visit, she confided in me, sharing things she had never mentioned to me before. She even urged me to draft a wedding guest list for my future marriage, despite there being no prospective groom on the horizon! The list contained over 100 guests, consisting of her relatives and friends from all corners of the world.

We had an incredible time during that final visit. My mother had travelled to more countries than anyone I had ever known, so she had an extensive network of acquaintances from all walks of life. I remember jokingly telling her, "Ima," meaning Mum, "this is so funny. I don't have anyone in my life right now, and I don't think I'll be getting married anytime soon anyway." She would laugh and respond, "Just write it down. I believe you'll be the first of my children to get married and have a wedding."

We even entered stationery shops to browse through wedding cards in the days that followed, continuing our light-hearted wedding discussions. She began selecting the ones she deemed the best cards for "my wedding," insisting, "One day you will get married, so it's better for us to prepare now." By personality, my mother was a perfectionist and a planner who would often have a daily 'to do list.' Therefore, the act of creating a wedding list was not foreign.

In the end, I decided to indulge her in this thought and let her dream of one of her daughters getting married soon. True to my mother's words, three years later, I did indeed get married, becoming the first of her daughters to walk down the aisle. Unfortunately, I embarked on the next chapter of my life without her walking by my side, as she was no longer there to witness that dream come true. I believe that in her own way, she foresaw it from a distance.

My mother consistently conveyed her preference for her children to enter marriage at age 25 or beyond, rather than at a younger age. She firmly believed that this age marked the commencement of personal maturity and self-discovery. In her view, anything younger was unsuitable for the solemn commitment of a lifelong marriage, further stating that it was paramount for young individuals to embark on a journey of self-discovery through education, and possibly travel and explore the world prior to embracing the commitment of marriage.

As fate would have it, I got married at the age of 27. My mother would have been overjoyed to have her wish fulfilled.

CHAPTER 5

THE LONG FLIGHT BACK HOME

Is this really happening? Please tell me it's just a joke... I'm trying to gather myself for the difficult journey back to Zambia. This has been one of the most challenging experiences of my life. As I mentioned earlier, my mother had worked for the airlines for many years, so my siblings and I were accustomed to flying alone. We always had the privilege of flying for free.

I vividly remember my mother's last visit to me, which took place a month before her passing. She gave me my air ticket for the year, as she always did. She would provide me with a ticket to keep just in case I needed to travel home urgently.

I can distinctly recall her words, "Mammy, here's your ticket in case there's an emergency back home." Mammy is a term of endearment. I smiled and replied, "Ima, what kind of emergency could possibly happen?" She smiled back and simply said, "You never know, just keep it safe." Oh, how little did I know that I would need that ticket sooner than I could have imagined.

Regrettably, in the midst of the shock, I was unable to locate my ticket. Two of my cousins had paid me a visit the previous day and decided to spend the night. We had stayed up late reminiscing and laughing through the night. As we were winding down in the early hours of the morning, we received the dreaded phone call. Looking back, I am glad I was not alone. That morning, other family friends who had heard about my mother's sudden passing came to offer their support before my flight to Zambia.

So, together, we all searched tirelessly in an attempt to find the missing ticket, but our efforts proved fruitless. All I could hear were the echoes of my mother's voice, repeating her words, "Mammy, here's your ticket; you never know, you might need it in case of an emergency." Little did I realize at the time that her words would ring true, though not in the way I had initially thought. I was now embarking on a journey, not to tend to an emergency, but to bid farewell to my beloved mother and my best friend, knowing that she would never hear my voice again.

My cousins lovingly accompanied me to the airport. The train ride to the airport felt surreal, as if I were trapped in a bewildering dream. I could not fathom the purpose of my journey to Zambia. I desperately wished that someone would tell me that this was all a terrible prank, but deep down, I knew it was an undeniable reality.

The journey to the airport stretched on endlessly as a whirlwind of questions swirled in my mind. My cousins, understanding my need for quiet support, remained by my side, offering their presence without uttering many words. I could not deal with any condolences because I did not actually accept that my mother was gone.

Fortunately, the airline staff had been informed by management about my urgent need to travel on the same day I received the news. Regardless of whether I had a ticket or not, they made arrangements for me to fly due to my mother's position within the company.

Upon reaching the airport, the airline staff showed remarkable kindness towards me, going above and beyond to assist. They granted me the privilege of flying first class, providing me with the best seat on the plane. This gesture was incredibly thoughtful, as it allowed me the space and comfort I needed to process the shock, unlike the cramped conditions of economy class.

I found myself seated next to a young girl who was eager to engage in conversation and requested that I draw pictures with her. Despite my desire to be left alone to grieve, I politely obliged. In hindsight, I suspect that the staff intentionally placed the little girl beside me. Since the first-class section wasn't fully occupied, she could have sat anywhere else. So, perhaps as a way to divert my attention from the shock and pain I was experiencing, they deemed it fitting.

It seemed that many of the staff on the plane were acquainted with my mother and recognized me as her daughter, hence their sensitivity and understanding were evident throughout the flight.

At one point, while on the plane and in deep soul anguish, I kept wishing that the plane would crash so I would not have to face what awaited me in Zambia. I did not have the strength to face anything or anyone. I found it hard to eat or drink; food became my enemy. No matter what was offered to me on the plane, I declined. I simply opted for an energy drink that I had brought with me. I now realize that at that time, I was in a state of shock.

I remember trying to sleep but failing because even sleep abandoned my eyes, leaving me in a pit of dark despair and hopelessness. I cannot adequately describe the emotions I was experiencing. It was a numb feeling, detached from the reality of what was happening around me.

I began to question God about the prayers for long life that I had made for my mother in previous years. I asked the common question that often arises during times of mourning: "Why, Lord? Why did it have to be my mother, and why now?" I pleaded with God, expressing how much my mother meant to me. "I cannot live without her," I confided in Him, silently shedding tears so as not to be seen by the little girl who was asleep nearby. Thankfully, it was late at night, and she had drifted off.

As I closed my eyes deep in thought, I witnessed something inexplicable, something I could not put into words. It was as if I saw my mother's spirit gracefully drifting among the clouds. She appeared blissful, and she expressed her remorse for not bidding me a proper farewell. "I am sorry that you were the only one of my children who was not there when I left, but I want you to know that you don't need to be sorrowful because where I am is a beautiful place, and I am at peace."

Opening my eyes, I pondered, "What was that? Was it a vision? Or what did I glimpse in the spiritual realm?" In that moment, I believe, and I realized that God was comforting me, assuring me that my mother was safe, and reminding me that she belonged to Him first, even before she became my mother.

However, even with that profound revelation, the sadness and pain of losing such a significant presence in my life persisted. I understood that my existence would never be the same without my mother's invaluable presence and influence.

I used to say that I lived for my mother, and truthfully, I had never known a love as profound as hers. Yet, what eluded me at the time was the realization that God was not obligated to explain His choices regarding His children. It was within His prerogative to keep her on Earth or to take her away.

The most difficult part for me was accepting God's actions. I felt a sense of injustice, questioning how He could allow the love of my life to vanish from my world when there was still so much, she had not witnessed her children achieve. It was a concept that proved challenging to comprehend.

CHAPTER 6

LET ME MOURN MY OWN WAY

The following day, upon my arrival in Zambia, I was greeted by a gathering of mourners eagerly awaiting my presence on the airport runway. Various relatives, both near and distant, had gathered there. Amidst the crowd, it was my younger sister who provided solace and comfort. My other two siblings remained at home with our grandparents, aunts, and uncles.

Seeing the multitude of people at the airport brought the realization even closer to home, confirming the truth of what I had dreaded and what had been relayed to me.

While in the car, I mustered the courage to ask if I could visit my mother and see her for myself. However, I was advised against it, given my fragile emotional state. Despite that, a part of me still could not fully accept the fact that she had departed so abruptly.

Upon arriving home, I was met with a scene of mourners in immense distress. My aunties, uncles, and grandmother were engulfed in sorrow. As soon as they laid eyes on me, they erupted into wails, exclaiming, "Your mother has left us; she is gone." My grandmother, with tears streaming down her face, gazed at me and uttered the heart-breaking words, "How are we going to manage without her?"

Witnessing my grandmother and beloved aunties in such agony was an intensely painful moment. It compelled me to momentarily shift my focus away from my own grief and observe the profound impact my mother's absence had on those around me.

Feeling a deep sense of detachment, I excused myself from the mourners and made my way to my mother's bedroom. In my desperate search for answers, I hoped that by being in her personal space, I would somehow uncover the truth and discover that this was all just a cruel joke.

Stepping into her room, everything appeared exactly as it had been the day before when she had returned from her work trip to South Africa. Her bag and work uniform remained untouched, as if she had merely gone out and would return to tidy up, just as she always did. I could not resist the urge to go further, to look through her belongings, yearning for a sign that she was still present in some way.

Once again, I approached one of my aunties with a plea to see her, only to be met with another rejection, denying me the opportunity to lay eyes on her once more.

I recall that my appetite had diminished greatly during those days. Despite the necessity of eating for physical strength, I discovered that food became an adversary when I was overwhelmed with distress. While some people turn to food for comfort in times of sadness, I found myself repelled by it when I was unhappy. The days of mourning eventually transitioned into funeral preparations, commonly referred to as a burial in Zambia.

During this period, in search of solace and strength, I would take my Bible and venture outdoors to find a secluded spot. There, in the quietness, I would pour out my heart to God, alone in my anguish, attempting to find hope in the words I read. However, I struggled to establish a connection with God, as I felt utterly broken.

Consequently, I decided to listen to worship music, to pray and cry and cry some more. Yet, I soon discovered that listening to my inspirational songs was prohibited during the mourning period, and out of respect for the elders, I obediently abstained. Nevertheless, restlessness consumed me, leaving me unsure of how to occupy myself. Since I was constantly surrounded by people, being alone for an extended period was deemed detrimental to my physical and mental well-being.

The elders' concerns stemmed from the belief that during deep mourning, individuals might be inclined to harm themselves, leading them to closely monitor those grieving. In the midst of this watchful environment, I found myself trapped in a tangle of confusion. Questions flooded my mind: What should I do now? Where should I go? How can I even allow myself to cry? My emotions held the reins, dictating my actions, and I felt a profound lack of control over my own life.

Denial consumed me entirely, even though it had been days since I received the devastating news and was surrounded by fellow mourners, mostly family and friends. I struggled to accept the harsh reality that my life had abruptly changed, and I no longer had my mother with me on this earthly plane. It felt impossible to fathom, and the truth of it all eluded me. It simply did not seem real.

Your mother has passed away! My mother? Shock beyond description hit me. I was speechless, confused, and still in denial as one mourner after another would come and repeat what seemed like the same senseless words.

Some of the comforters who approached me repeated phrases like "don't worry, it's okay don't cry, be strong" However, these voices became a discord of harsh sounds echoing in my mind, resembling endless reverberations in a cave. I longed to release a scream and weep until my strength was depleted the weight of anguish I carried felt unbearably suffocating, trapping my soul in torment.

Amidst the multitude of well-meaning but misguided comforters, I found no solace or genuine hope, only a clamour like the clashing of loud cymbals. Their whispers seemed to be filled with meaningless words. In my introverted nature, I listened to them out of respect, acknowledging their sincere attempts to offer support. Yet, some of their words of comfort rang hollow, being profoundly wrong, inappropriate, and difficult to believe.

I vividly remember an encounter with an elderly Christian woman who approached me with well- intentioned words She said, "My dear, you have cried enough, when you cry like this, you are grieving the Holy Spirit." I was taken aback by her statement, feeling a jolt in my stomach as I looked at her with a mixture of confusion and disbelief. How could my expression of deep sorrow possibly grieve the Holy Spirit, especially when He understands the immense pain I am experiencing? I questioned within myself the true meaning behind grieving the Holy Spirit. Although I acknowledge her good intentions, looking back on that moment, I now realize that her words lacked true godly wisdom and biblical understanding. I can still recall another encounter with another Christian woman who attempted to empathize with my pain. She said, "Namakau, I know how you feel; I lost a child, so I know the pain of losing a loved one, and therefore I understand what you are going through." I looked at her and allowed her words to resonate in my mind.

As a contemplative individual, I felt the urge to respond by saying, "You don't know how I feel. I have just lost my mother. Your loss was different; you lost a baby." However, out of respect for my mother's teachings, I remained silent and chose not to retort. It was during these moments that I began to realize that people often felt compelled to offer a word of comfort, even if it was not necessarily applicable to the specific situation. With maturity, you learn that in such moments all you need in the form of comfort is just to know that loved ones are present in the moment, even when they have nothing to say…it is okay not to utter a single word but simply offer a hug or wipe one's tears instead.

I decided that the voices I was hearing were not helping me; it was clear to me that I had to swiftly retreat and seek solace in a secluded and silent space. I longed to find a sanctuary where I could begin to comprehend the profound sorrow within my heart and shut out the presence of others. In that place of solitude, I desired to engage in heartfelt conversations with God, openly expressing my pain, confusion, and deep anguish of soul through lamentation.

It was disheartening to realize that even among fellow Christians, their continuous flow of endless, meaningless, and futile words only added to my distress. These words lacked the wisdom, positivity, and maturity I so desperately sought.

So, leaving me alone in my anguish and pain was probably the best thing they could have done for me. Again, I recall a distant relative who came to offer her condolences. All she said was, "Namakau, I am so sorry. I have no words; I am just so sorry and shocked." I felt a deep empathy in those words. It seemed like finally; someone truly understood my pain. It was as if she had gently poured fresh oil on my wound and was diligently nursing me back to health.

I deeply appreciated those words. She didn't say much but chose to sit silently beside me for some time. It was wise of her not to offer misguided advice like some others had done. She simply acknowledged her own feelings, and that was sufficient. I must say she was one of the most sensible sources of comfort I encountered. Her words have stayed with me, and I haven't forgotten them.

Sometimes, when someone is grieving, they don't need an abundance of comforting words. Empathy is invaluable, and a hug is precious. Words lacking wisdom and understanding can potentially do more harm than good.

Although people may have believed they were helping by offering sympathy, during my time of grief, I sometimes wished I had been given the space to mourn in my own way. For example, someone else who has lost a parent might express their own sentiments and say, "I know how it feels; I lost a mother too." The truth is, we cannot fully understand how someone else feels, even if we have had a similar experience. Each person's pain and grief are unique, influenced by their individual circumstances and the relationship they had with the deceased.

In some cases, losing a mother may not be as devastating for one person as it is for another, because circumstances and relationships vary. In my situation, losing my mother left me completely shattered and displaced because she played the pivotal role of both my father and mother, and as I mentioned earlier, she was my entire world.

CHAPTER 7

THE LOSS

Writing about my experience has been incredibly challenging, even after all these years. The loss of my mother remains a sensitive subject, depending on the circumstances. Sometimes, I find it easy and painless to describe the experience without tears, while other times, it feels quite sore as if it just happened yesterday.

The impact can still be felt differently during significant milestones in life, and certain life experiences serve as stark reminders of the loss.

In the early stages of grieving, the wound felt raw and too painful to even touch. It seemed as though I was reliving the entire ordeal. I still struggled with the use of the title "the late" when referring to a deceased loved one. Using the term "dead" to describe my mother felt almost taboo. I would become angry with anyone who referred to her as "the body" of "the late." Initially, such references made me cringe.

I didn't want to hear them and found them unnecessary because every individual is unique. Whether alive or deceased, there can only ever be one such person, and therefore, they should be referred to simply as themselves, not as the "late." In my opinion, it is totally unnecessary.

I personally prefer to simply call people by their names, even after they have departed. I have never quite understood the purpose of these titles, and I still hold that sentiment.

The memory of a loved one lives on in the hearts and minds of those who cared for them. I rarely hear my family members referring to my deceased mother as "dead." Nor do I hear people whose parents have passed away referring to them as "my dead mother" or "my dead father."

While some individuals may use such terms, I personally feel uncomfortable doing so. Most often, I find people refer to their loved ones who have passed away as "my mom," "my dad," "my brother," or "my sister," followed by the phrase "the late" and their name. They choose to remember them by their names. Perhaps in some families, these titles are used I am unsure. I believe it ultimately comes down to what feels comfortable for each individual.

During conversations, when I mention the name of a loved one who has passed away, I typically refer to them by their name and people usually understand who I am referring to, there is often no confusion, even if there are others with the same name. Thus, I find it unnecessary to use the term "the late" when referring to my departed mother. After all, her name still resonates in history. She remains alive in my memories, and she will never be the "late" to me, though departed. Her influence continues on through me as her DNA is a part of who I am. I am a product of her life, as she gave birth to me.

My main point here is that the pain of losing someone you love never truly fades away. Though they may be gone from the Earth's plane, and many people may forget their existence, but to you, they remain a significant part of your life and continue to live on. It is up to you to carry on living and find new ways to cope with their absence in your life.

There are certain things in life that one may never truly get over; instead, they learn to rebuild and live again after experiencing a tragedy. It is through the pain endured that individuals discover an incredible capacity for growth and develop the ability to offer support to others facing similar circumstances.

Although there may still be moments when one requires support, particularly during significant milestones that would typically involve the presence of the departed loved one, they can extend the gift of their presence to someone else in need.

Moreover, I personally found that once I accepted my loss and worked towards moving beyond the grieving phase, I discovered a remarkable sense of grace and resilience to cope with the immense pain. Despite the anguish that lingered within the depths of my soul, I made a conscious choice to find peace with my loss and accept it as a part of my past. Simultaneously, I strive to forge ahead and seek solace in the present moment.

Perhaps, like me, you hold a spiritual perspective on death and dying, believing that even though the physical body of a loved one may have departed from this Earth, their spirit continues to exist and never truly dies. This belief has provided me with immense comfort. In my view, the most beautiful aspect is the assurance that, if our loved ones have passed away in Christ, we will have the opportunity to see them again. This realization brings profound solace.

While I may not have mourned in the way I initially expected, I discovered a renewed connection with God. I embarked on a fresh and vibrant journey, walking alongside the God of the universe who aided me in accepting my loss. He promised to be by my side as I navigate life without the guiding influence, counsel, and love of my mother.

CHAPTER 8

LORD, THIS HURTS SO MUCH!

My constant reminder nowadays is that regardless of how much we love our families or friends, they do not fully belong to us; they are merely on loan in our lives. I liken these relationships to people coming and going in a busy airport, transient passengers in my life. Their Maker may decide to take them at any time, just as it was in the case of the biblical account of Job.

Job's faith was tested beyond natural human ability when suddenly without warning, a windstorm struck the four corners of his son's house, resulting in the tragic death of all ten of his children in a single day.

Although Job learned many lessons along the way, I often wonder how I would have reacted in such a situation. Job experienced the devasting loss of all his material possessions, children, rejection from his wife, and physical agony. In the midst of his suffering, Job was visited by three friends who intended to comfort him, but due to their lack of wisdom they accused him of transgression, linking that to his suffering.

However, it is difficult to fathom how anyone could ever endure such agonizing and overwhelming circumstances. Personally, I can't imagine how I would cope with such a catastrophic situation.

Job's initial reaction was one of extreme grief and sorrow, which is only natural given the magnitude of his losses. However, what struck me about Job was that he still chose to worship God despite the numerous other disasters that befell him. Job's incredible strength of character and resilience serve as a testament to his unwavering faith in God, even in the face of unimaginable hardships. This aspect of Job's story continues to inspire and resonate with many people to this day.

On the day we laid my mother to rest, her relatives entered the bedroom to select a dress for her, unaware that we, her children, had already made that decision. Some less considerate family members began insisting on taking her makeup, perfume, and a special blanket to adorn her with.

I vividly recall expressing to those relatives that these material things were not of great importance. While it may have been acceptable to apply makeup on her, why the perfume, and why wrap her in her lovely pink blanket?

I asked one of those relatives if all the requested items were truly necessary. They claimed that their intentions were to give her a dignified burial, but deep down, I knew their motives were selfish and malevolent. We firmly refused to allow them to take anything that my siblings and I deemed irrelevant.

I remember tearfully expressing, "My mother is gone, and you want to spray perfume on her body?" I felt that these relatives did not genuinely care about our loss; they simply wanted to seize what they could and benefit where they had not sown.

Despite being emotionally distressed, I remained acutely aware of the activities unfolding around me. My siblings and I would not allow them to disrespect our feelings or tarnish the memory of our mother. In that moment, I could not care less about what anyone thought because we, her children, understood her better than these relatives who were virtually strangers to us.

The atmosphere of the room felt lighter when they finally departed, and I silently shed tears once again, overwhelmed by disbelief at the situation unfolding before me. All I longed for was solitude, free from the burdensome presence of relatives who had never truly cared for us, even when our mother was alive.

Later, I discovered that some of those very relatives were actually pleased that we were left orphaned. I overheard comments like, "We will see how they will suffer now that their mother is gone; no more travelling abroad for them." It was painful to hear such words from people who were supposed to be our family.

In those moments, I recalled the words of my grandmother, which she often shared with us when we were younger. She would say, "You think all these people love you for you; on the contrary, they only love you because of your mother's career and what honour it brings them, and even more so what they gain from the relationship. If you were poor, they would not even look at you or consider you at all."

As a little girl, I could not understand why my grandmother would say such harsh things about our relatives. I thought, "How could she speak so negatively about our own family?" However, little did I realize that she had lived a much longer life than I had and had gained wisdom through her own experiences. Over the years, my grandmother's words resonated within me. I began to question and realized that she was right about many things.

As a child, I could not fully appreciate her advice, and the idea of having enemies within the family seemed far-fetched. Yet, I now understand that my grandmother was trying to impart the truth about life and people, whether we were ready to hear it or not. While we did not fully value her wisdom at the time, but as I grew older, I became increasingly grateful for her blunt yet insightful guidance.

CHAPTER 9

SAYING GOODBYE

"Someone, please wake me up from this nightmare I'm experiencing." I desperately wished that it was just a nightmare. The day I will never forget had finally arrived, and it still felt like a cruel joke. A flashback from my childhood surfaced in my mind, reminding me of a prank I had played on my mother when I was in primary school.

It happened one April Fool's Day when she came to pick up my sisters and me. I had decided to trick her by pretending that she had a flat tyre. Mum believed me and got out of the car, filled with panic as she checked for the supposed issue. Then, with a burst of laughter, I exclaimed, "April Fool's Day!" Initially, my mother wasn't overly amused, but as she asked for the date, I proudly declared, "Ima, it's April Fool's Day!" She burst into laughter, amazed at how I had managed to play such a prank on her and how she fell for it.

Upon inspecting her car, my mother realized that she didn't actually have a flat tyre. As we all got into the car to leave the school premises, she expressed her relief that it was just a joke.

Whenever I would bring up that prank and remind her of her response, how she believed me and stepped out of the car to investigate the flat tyre, we would laugh together, cherishing the memory. But now, those fond memories and laughter would be mine alone, as she was no longer with us.

This sorrowful day was nothing like an "April Fool's Day" or any other day I may have pranked my mother. I was still in a state of shock, a purely human emotion. How does one cope when their world shatters? It's the moment when the once secure and familiar world becomes unfamiliar and unsettling.

Grief engulfed me, an agonizing and God-given emotion. What does one do when their heart is breaking? In that moment, I remembered the words from the Bible, "Jesus wept." Jesus Christ had experienced grief, loss, and felt every human emotion when his friend Lazarus died, who He later raised from the dead. Jesus was a man acquainted with sorrow, for He carried our griefs and sorrows when He died on the cross.

I struggled with the "why" question. What does one do when they don't understand why? Even Jesus Himself asked the "why" question when He cried out to God on the cross in distress, saying, "My God, why have you forsaken me?" Sometimes, we may ask "why" and not receive an answer. Similarly, Jesus understood that He had to die and then rise from the dead, but on that cross, there was a profound silence from God.

What a night it was... I couldn't find much sleep, and how could I? How would life be from this point onward? What would this day hold for me? I couldn't help but wonder what my future would look like. Oh, the uncertainty weighed heavily on my soul, and the grief in my heart felt unbearably heavy. Could someone please wake me up from this? Is this some cruel joke? A never-ending nightmare? Is it truly happening to me? All those stories about people losing loved ones seemed distant until now when it had struck my own family.

One can handle death when it befalls others, but when it stares you directly in the face, it leaves you utterly devastated. How did we end up here? My mother, truly gone just like that?

I remember how she used to playfully talk about her own funeral, and we, her children, would often tell her, "Ima, stop talking like that." Now, the reality had mercilessly arrived. I found myself going back to her bedroom, gazing at her personal belongings with disbelief, still in denial of the harsh truth.

During that long and painful day, I kept wishing someone would wake me up from the nightmare of saying goodbye to the person I loved dearly. Unfortunately, this was not a cruel joke or a haunting nightmare. It was the harsh reality.

How will I find the strength to carry on after this day, LORD? I whispered under my breath, uncertain if I could endure this torment. Could I request to be exempt from this day and this pain? So many questions swirled in my mind, filled with ifs, buts, and how's. Why did this have to happen?

Yet, as I walked around the house that morning, witnessing my family's preparations, I realized that I was not the only one struggling and suffering under the weight of the imminent loss we were about to face. It was a collective heartbreak and loss for all those who were close to my mother.

Pacing around the house that morning, I witnessed two of my aunties completely devastated, weeping inconsolably in each other's embrace. One of them said, "I cannot bear this pain and loss today. She was my best friend and my sister. I have no strength to say goodbye."

It was in that moment that it dawned on me that my grandmother had lost her youngest daughter, my uncles had lost a sister, my aunties had lost a sister, friends had lost a dear friend, her cousins had lost a beloved elder cousin, nieces and nephews had lost an aunt, grandchildren had lost their grandmother, work colleagues had lost an exceptional mentor, and we, her children had lost our mother . It was a profound blow that pierced all our hearts at different levels of relationship. However challenging the task may be, we knew we had to gather the strength to lay her to rest.

Saying goodbye to my mother was the most difficult task I had ever faced in my entire life. It shattered my heart into countless fragments. Even though the hours to the burial were approaching, I remained in a state of shock and denial until the moment my siblings and I could visit the funeral parlour to see her one last time.

As my eyes fell upon my mother's lifeless form, I could not help but gaze at her with a mix of emotions. She appeared serene, as if peacefully immersed in a deep slumber. Her features were undisturbed, her hair neatly arranged, and everything seemed to be in perfect order.

I could not believe my eyes as I stared at her in the casket. It was difficult to comprehend that it was truly her. My thoughts raced, "Ima, so we spent our last month together, and I had no idea it would be our final farewell. When we said goodbye on that last day at Aldgate East in London, as you headed to the hotel to prepare for your journey back home, little did I know that I would never see you alive again."

Life felt incredibly cruel and unjust in that moment. Yet, as I observed my mother's appearance, she looked just as I had seen her a month earlier in London. Her beauty remained unblemished. She was elegantly dressed in her work uniform, the one we had chosen for her to wear as a symbol of pride and honour. Though she was cold to the touch, her essence had not faded.

In that moment, a realization slowly sank in, and I found myself acknowledging the painful truth that she was truly gone from this world. Still in a state of shock, distress, and denial, I couldn't shake the profound impact of what I had just witnessed. I wished for a resurrection miracle, as Lazarus in the Bible had experienced.

As we left the funeral parlour and made our way to the church, I observed the activities unfolding around me. The church service seemed to proceed smoothly, but I must confess that my focus was solely consumed by grief and loss, my eyes fixated on the coffin before us.

The details of the service hardly registered as they offered me little solace. After the church ceremony concluded, we made our way to the final resting place, known as the Leopards Hill Cemetery. The sight that greeted us on the journey was staggering. The convoy of cars accompanying us was beyond anything I could have imagined. It felt surreal to witness such a grand procession. To say that my mother received a dignified burial would be an understatement.

Despite the immense pain for our family, she was given an awe-inspiring farewell, with a procession of cars and police escorts accompanying us throughout the journey. I had never witnessed anything like it for any of our previously departed family members. I was left in awe, unsure of where all these prominent individuals and the extensive entourage of vehicles had come from.

As I whispered to myself, engaged in silent conversations within my mind, I couldn't help but express my thoughts to my dear departed mother, "Ima, you would have been amazed by your funeral. The number of cars and people in attendance to bid you farewell was beyond belief."

The event had been meticulously organized by the older members of our family, and it turned out to be a truly remarkable tribute to her. They had done an outstanding job in ensuring that her send-off was nothing short of spectacular.

However, it saddens me to reflect that since the time of writing this book, many other close family members who laid my mother to rest have also passed away.

In the past, my mother would occasionally bring up the topic of her funeral in a casual and light- hearted manner. Despite my discomfort with such discussions, she would playfully express her wishes, saying, "I know that I will depart before you, my children, because God knows I could never bear the pain of burying any of you." These conversations about death were never my favourite, and even now, they still weigh heavily on me. However, she would humorously add that she wanted us to dress up and celebrate her life at her funeral, encouraging us not to mourn as those who have no hope.

As I replayed those conversations about her death in my mind, a flood of questions and confusion overwhelmed me. I couldn't comprehend why it had to happen so soon. My mother was still young, with just a few years left until she turned 50, and yet she was taken away from us just like that. Coming to terms with this reality was incredibly challenging.

I found it impossible to dress up, apply makeup, or wear the hats she had wanted for her funeral. My heart was shattered, consumed by grief and a profound sense of loss. All I longed for was to have her back by my side. However, some of my aunties and other family members respected her wishes and adorned themselves as she would have wanted.

At the cemetery, I noticed a multitude of flowers piled upon her grave, but in that moment of pain and sorrow, I couldn't bring myself to care about who had laid what size wreath. All I desired was the return of my mother. Reflecting on it now, I wish all those flowers could have been brought to her when she could still appreciate their fragrance and beauty.

As I grow older and experience more of life, I never cease to be saddened by how the deceased are celebrated as heroes after their passing, while often going unnoticed and unappreciated during their time on Earth. It is a tragic reality, and it speaks to the shortcomings of our humanity. Should we not appreciate those who are alive more than the dead who no longer see, feel, hear, touch, or sense?

We gave my mother a remarkable send-off, and I was astounded by her popularity. The presence of a police escort in the convoy of cars highlighted the extent of her impact. It was surprising to learn that her position in the airline commanded such respect in society. The grandeur of the funeral truly befitted a hero.

Despite her accomplishments, my mother was always humble and never flaunted her status. Those who knew her at work acknowledged her steadfast dedication and strong leadership. I had no idea how much love and admiration she had earned, which I believe would have been a source of joy for her had she known this in her lifetime.

On the day of the burial, I witnessed the true significance of my mother's life and the profound impact she had on others. As her daughter, I often overlooked the numerous lives she had touched silently, without seeking recognition. There were many individuals, unknown to me, who held my mother in such high regard as their boss, mentor, and benefactor in times of need. While at home, she was simply "Ima" to us, not the Chief Inflight Inspector of a national airline.

Now I realize that she wore multiple hats and left a lasting impression on numerous people.

CHAPTER 10

FACING GRIEF

Two months later, with my wounds still festering, I returned to England. I had not realized that grieving was a lengthy process, and this was only the beginning. I had thought that coming back to England would be a good way to confront my heartache and everything that had happened in Zambia so I could begin to move forward. However, to my surprise, grief took hold of me in another peculiar manner.

The first realization was the undeniable fact that I would never see my mother in this life again. Mum used to visit my sisters and me in England, but now there were no more visits, no letters, no birthday cards, as there used to be, and no more phone calls. As the months went by, her absence became increasingly noticeable and painful.

Each passing month intensified my desperation to see her again, even though I was fully aware that it was no longer possible.

This profound longing led me into a state of deep sadness and depression. At that time, I had no prior understanding of what trauma truly looked or felt like.

The passing of a loved one can be intensely difficult and painful, though I have learned that not every loss leads to trauma, because people process grief differently.

As time went on, a profound void started to form within my heart. The painful sensation of missing my mother became increasingly overwhelming.

In the early stages of grief, the circumstances surrounding her death may have felt significant, but as time passed, I came to realize that the manner of her passing held less importance. Regardless of how she had died, the pain and emptiness remained constant. When someone passes away, the nature of the relationship undergoes a transformation rather than coming to an abrupt end. It transitions from a face-to- face connection to one that exists through internalized living memories, stories, and the legacy they leave behind. Through personal experience, I have come to understand that grief is a transformative process. It is through pain that we grow and evolve.

In a paradoxical way, grief becomes necessary as it guides us to adapt and manage the pain, ultimately shaping a new version of ourselves. The grief process serves as a teacher, showing us how to reconstruct our world in the absence of our loved one. While the grief itself may endure for years, it becomes triggered by different events over time, although the intensity of the pain tends to diminish.

However, the loss of a loved one creates a profound emptiness in our world, and grieving becomes a long- term process as we navigate through this void. As we progress through grief, the once unbearable pain gradually becomes more manageable.

It is worth noting that individuals with strong faith, supportive families, and good friends often find it easier to cope with grief. The connections we forge with others are vital in life.

These connections provide us with a sense of belonging and support, enabling us to function properly. When there is a disconnection or rupture in these relationships, it can greatly impact our ability to function effectively. Recognizing the importance of connection and nurturing meaningful relationships can play a significant role in navigating the journey of grief and rebuilding our lives.

My mother passed away on the 3rd of April 1993. As December of that year approached, it became evident that Christmas would be a lonely one. The realization hit me that this would be the first Christmas without her, and I could not fathom what the festive season would be like without hearing her voice wishing me a merry Christmas and offering best wishes for the New Year.

Thankfully, that year Christmas arrived and passed with a sense of calmness and even some amazing moments filled with fond memories of my mother. Consequently, it wasn't as dreadful as I had initially anticipated.

However, the following year marked the quiet culmination of my battle with depression. I never shared this with anyone because, at that time, I did not even realize that what I was experiencing was depression. It felt like an enduring sorrow deep within my heart that lasted for days on end. The peculiar aspect was that it resembled grief more than mere prolonged sadness, even though it exhibited all the symptoms associated with depression such as hopelessness, feeling unhappy, suicide ideation, worry, anxiety, insomnia, stress and finding no pleasure in things that I once enjoyed. It was a prolonged deep sadness that mirrored grief in its nature.

What I know now is that had I decided to visit the General Practitioner (GP) clinic, I would have probably received a diagnosis for depression and would perhaps have been put on medication. Since I understood the root cause of the sadness and hopelessness, I believed that I could somehow exert control over my situation.

Consequently, I carried on with life and soldiered through, conforming to the expectations of societal norms and those around me. At that time, I wasn't aware that there exists a fine line distinguishing between grief and depression. I had no awareness that seeking bereavement counselling might have potentially helped me navigate and process my pain more effectively.

In my culture, mental health issues, anxiety, including depression, were rarely addressed as legitimate conditions. This stigma surrounding mental health was deeply ingrained within my family, friends, and society at large. Individuals facing depression or any mental health challenges were often met with scorn and had their dignity stripped away.

Moreover, within many Christian circles, depression was considered non-existent. It was believed that as Christians, we were followers of Jesus Christ and therefore somewhat immune to the unfortunate circumstances of life. It was also believed that we possessed the power to overcome life's challenges victoriously. While there is truth in this belief, I hasten to say that there are instances where it is encouraged to seek professional help for prolonged mental health challenges.

Therefore, as a result, mental health became a taboo topic, leaving individuals like me without the necessary support, knowledge and understanding. Through my experience, I have learned that grief in the context of bereavement is a lengthy and chronic process, often accompanied by triggers along the way. Seeking grief counselling allows one to bring their sadness to the surface and facilitates a unique journey of dealing with loss.

I have come to understand that, despite their good intentions, people may sometimes say foolish, senseless, or insensitive things in an attempt to provide consolation to someone who is grieving. It is crucial to recognize that individuals cope with grief in their own unique ways. Therefore, it is important to share our own experiences and perspectives without imposing our coping methods on others, unless specifically requested.

Each person's grief journey is deeply personal, and what may be helpful for one individual may not be the same for another. Furthermore, respecting and honouring individual differences in grieving processes is essential in offering support and understanding to those who are grieving.

Sometimes, simply mourning with the bereaved is all that truly matters, rather than trying to fix or solve things. In grief counselling, listening attentively and validating their pain is a vital aspect of demonstrating empathy. Although our loved ones may have passed away, referring to them in the present tense rather than the past can be helpful for those still grappling with the loss.

The relationship they shared with their loved one remains current and relevant to them. Hence, respecting and acknowledging this perspective is an integral part of supporting the bereaved during their transition and healing process.

I have also come to understand that grief and trauma can manifest in different ways. Some individuals experience grief due to the loss of a business, a marriage, a house, a job, a pet, a dream, or other significant aspects of their lives. While there may be similarities between grieving for the deceased and grieving for the attachment to things, there are subtle differences. Although the intensity of grief may be heightened when a loved one passes away, it doesn't necessarily diminish over time but rather transforms as it is repeatedly processed.

In the initial stage of loss, a range of emotions emerges, such as anger, hurt, a sense of being defeated, and a numbing sensation. The denial phase is commonly experienced regardless of the type of grief one faces. It is a natural response to protect oneself from the overwhelming reality of loss.

However, a grieving person knows what they need. They may not need grief counselling just yet because grief is a journey, and everyone's grief process is different, as already mentioned. We must respect that. Once the loss occurs, it is tragic and often followed by a painful and lengthy grief process. Again, it's important to understand that everyone's grief is unique, so offering comfort in generalities can sometimes be a disservice to the person who is grieving. We must be respectful of everyone's unique response to grief.

You don't get over loss and grief, in my opinion when people say, "Get over it!" I am often left dumbfounded by those words. How do you get over a deeply distressing experience? Show me how. We are human beings with real emotions and feelings.

Therefore, the scars resulting from severe emotional, mental, or physical injuries remain and serve as constant reminders of what grief or trauma did to us and left behind. So, you don't fully recover from grief or trauma; rather, you gain mastery over it. You take it with you, and it becomes integrated with who you are. Without making it an altar or an idol, you learn to rule your own spirit well, even when you are broken. You learn new ways of coping with loss. Two people may suffer a similar loss but may not necessarily recover from the experience in the same way simply because they share it. Each individual must learn how to cope with their unique situation.

The confusion surrounding loss left me to deal with my heartache and grief alone for some time until I was able to confide in some good friends. These friends offered a listening ear, although they didn't fully have the capacity to put the pieces of the broken puzzle together. I appreciated their empathetic support, which was all I needed at the time, as my immediate family was in Zambia. Therefore, there was no one in England whom I could truly talk to and who fully understood the extent of the grief I experienced.

CHAPTER 11

UNEXPRESSED EMOTIONS

My journey would not be complete if all I share with you are my life's woes, the doom and gloom; I also want to share moments of joy. However, it is crucial that you understand that human beings, regardless of their public portrayal, experience real pain. What we often witness is a mirage, and it may not always reflect reality or truth. Social media has played a role in amplifying lies and falsehoods. It only presents what people want you to see about their lives. Most of the time, it doesn't capture the true picture of real-life events.

The joys of life are sometimes overshadowed by prolonged periods of sadness. However, even in the midst of ugliness, there is goodness.

To navigate the grief process and shake off the depression that had consumed me for months, I made a conscious decision to start living again, even when I felt emotionally dead. It didn't matter how I appeared on the outside because I had become skilled at hiding my pain. What mattered was finding a renewed sense of purpose in life.

In early 1994, I made the choice to join the church evangelistic gospel choir to keep myself occupied while working part-time. Little did I know that grief would strike once again. No one had ever told me that grief and trauma unfold in different stages and involve a process of unpacking sorrows and addressing them whenever the wounds resurface. Working through these stages took time and patience.

So, as I was ploughing my way through those healing stages, I found myself grappling to understand the whirlwind of emotions that had become my life. It felt like one moment I was holding it together, and the next I would crumble, left to carefully gather the shattered pieces of my existence. The initial stages consisted of shock, numbness, and denial. I could not comprehend the reality of losing my mother. Disbelief and denial enveloped me as I struggled to accept the truth.

Following the initial shock, excruciating pain and guilt washed over me. I carried the weight of not being present when my mother passed away, which fuelled my anguish. Anger also emerged, although I didn't know where to direct it. I could not blame God, or could I? I understood that He did not delight in the suffering that befalls us, yet I grappled with a sense of disappointment, feeling that somehow God could have prevented my mother's sudden death. So, in a way, I felt let down by God.

While I hold the belief that God is love, I couldn't help but question where love resided in the act of taking away my mother.

I understood that God acts according to His own will, without apology or explanation to us mortals. However, I also recognized that sometimes Christians misinterpret the doctrine of God's Sovereignty, assuming a sense of powerlessness and attributing everything solely to God's control.

This complexity overwhelmed me as numerous unanswered questions flooded my mind. Nevertheless, I remained steadfast in my choice to prioritize the Holy Bible as the ultimate source of truth above any church doctrine alone. I sought to verify the alignment of any belief with the teachings of the Bible, ensuring it aligned with God's truth before endorsing it. This approach served as my compass amidst the uncertainties and allowed me to navigate the complexities of my faith.

In relation to the passing of my mother, I am aware and comprehend, based on my younger sister's account of events, that she firmly believes our mother would still be alive if she had received the necessary medical care and prompt attention upon her arrival at the hospital after experiencing a massive stroke.

I too believe that she would have survived; therefore, this was due to human medical negligence rather than the sovereignty of God. Yes, God is omnipotent, but He also grants power, knowledge, understanding, wisdom, authority, and dominion to humanity so that they can exercise it in the Earth. Thus, in my opinion, what happened to my mother was a result of medical negligence.

While many may argue with me on this point and claim that God allowed it, I respectfully disagree. This is my personal account, and it is my responsibility to recount how the events unfolded and how they were interpreted by me.

My siblings were present with my mother at the time of her passing and witnessed what occurred, so I trust that their account was accurate. I am aware that many individuals have faced similar situations where their loved ones have tragically succumbed to medical negligence and then attributed it to God.

However, in our case, I cannot place all the blame on God—perhaps some, but certainly not all.

As mentioned earlier, before I digressed, grief began to resurface, and with each passing day, I found myself missing my mother more and more.

In hindsight, I hadn't fully comprehended the significance of her frequent visits. Those precious moments of bonding and catching up were priceless. Therefore, her passing created a tremendous void in my life. I gradually started to confront the loneliness that accompanied the absence of a mother who was also a dear and faithful friend.

The most challenging phase was reaching the turning point of acceptance and finding hope. At that time, it seemed impossible to rebuild my life. Hope felt distant, and I was painfully aware of the constant denial I clung to, refusing to believe that my mother was truly gone. Although the initial shock had subsided, I realized I had not fully embraced my loss nor properly mourned my mother in the way I desired or should have.

During the mourning period in Zambia, our family house was constantly filled with people, leaving me with little opportunity to reflect and effectively process what had occurred. This lack of solitude prevented me from giving myself the necessary time to mourn and accept the loss in a way that would have been beneficial for my healing and progress towards moving forward.

After returning to my life in England, I came to the realization that despite being physically back in familiar surroundings, I was still trapped in a state of disbelief and denial. As a result, I found it challenging to fully let go of the grief and trauma that weighed upon me. However, I didn't fully understand that by allowing myself to release these emotions, I could initiate the healing process that was essential for my well-being.

I recall a particular day when I was attending choir practice, attempting to portray strength and composure in front of others. However, deep inside, I was on the verge of tears, wrestling with unresolved issues that plagued me. These were matters I deemed messy, and throughout my grieving process, I had learned to compartmentalize them as secrets, believing they had no bearing on other aspects of my life. I convinced myself that I had complete control over my emotions and would only reveal what I wanted others to see. The hard parts of my life began to show up in ways that I could not have imagined.

My past began to unravel, gradually exposing a series of suppressed emotions, catching me off guard. It was as if these unexpressed feelings were being introduced to the surface in ways I had not anticipated.

On that particular day, a lady pastor noticed my sombre mood and kindly inquired about my well- being. Her caring and soothing tone struck a chord within me, causing tears to well up and eventually leading to a complete emotional breakdown. I realized that I could not simply respond with a polite "I'm fine" because deep down, I knew I wasn't. The floodgates opened, and I cried uncontrollably as she embraced me tightly. In that moment, I came to understand the profound need I had to release my emotions through tears in order for my healing to commence. It was as if a heavy weight that I had been carrying had begun to be lifted, albeit only slightly.

My unexpected breakdown and the outpouring of tears caught me by surprise, leaving me astonished at myself and the depth of what I had been harbouring within me exposed.

The overwhelming sense of loss, displacement, and abandonment that I had experienced since my mother's passing had never been given the space it deserved for grief to be expressed in a truly beneficial manner.

It was on that same day, during choir practice, when the compassionate female pastor engaged in a conversation with me, providing an opportunity for me to express my emotions. She encouraged me to seek support from one of the church counsellors, emphasizing the importance of simply talking to someone about my feelings. Although I agreed to the suggestion, unfortunately, I never followed through with making an appointment.

At the time, I convinced myself that I would be fine after that emotional episode. It was surprising to me because in all that time, with all that I had been through, it occurred to me that I had not talked about my experience with anyone.

It is true that when we are grieving, we often focus on expressing how much we miss our loved ones, but we tend to overlook discussing our own feelings and the pain felt with those around us.

That brief conversation I had with the female pastor felt like a catalyst that opened a floodgate of emotions. It served as an invitation to openly express my pain and granted me the space to grieve in my own unique way.

In society, there can be an unspoken expectation to swiftly move on from the loss of a loved one after the funeral, as if we are supposed to forget them and the entire experience. However, this notion couldn't be farther from the reality of grief. We must allow ourselves to fully grieve and acknowledge our pain. It is crucial that, amidst the trauma, we remember to reach out and talk to someone who genuinely cares about our well-being.

Grief is an essential part of our healing journey, and we must learn to navigate it while continuing to live. It is about finding the strength to carry on, even in the midst of our pain, rather than allowing ourselves to merely exist under the weight of sorrow.

Grief is also the ability to listen to our emotions by admitting what they are, and how we really feel without fear.

You can speak to the raging storms of life by first acknowledging their presence, and then freeing yourself from being carried away by the tempest. For example, it is okay to feel afraid, but you can also declare that you are stronger than your fears. It is okay to say you are grieving right now, but you are also hopeful for the future. Likewise, it is okay to admit that you feel angry, but you choose joy and peace instead. So, sometimes it helps to name your emotions by paying close attention to the language of your heart.

Admitting how you really feel takes courage and it is strength, not weakness.

CHAPTER 12

ACCEPTING A NEW REALITY

The year was coming to an end once again, and I still hadn't made time to see the church counsellor. Somehow, I convinced myself that I was fine, especially on busy days when I didn't dwell on grief and loss. The type of trauma I was experiencing ran deep, leaving me with a profound sense of abandonment, loss, and defeat in the face of life's challenges.

My usual response was to push the pain aside, burying it in a corner of my heart and pretending it didn't exist until it resurfaced and hurt me again. Then I would briefly tend to the wound, only to cover it up once more.

Throughout this struggle, I would talk to God as if He were a friend I saw face-to-face, but I never asked Him to step into my pain and provide assistance. I would simply discuss it with Him, expressing how much I missed my mother. I would also continue to question why my mother had left us.

However, reflecting on my understanding of grief today, I realize that I should have asked God for help, healing, strength, renewed hope, and his guiding light to shine amidst the surrounding darkness instead of wallowing in deep anguish.

Although I now know that God fulfilled all these roles for me—my helper, my strength, my hope, my healer, and my guiding light—every step of the way, even when I could not perceive His presence. He was always there.

Accepting my new reality required me to acknowledge that even though I had experienced the various stages of grief over time, in order to move forward in a constructive manner, I needed to surrender the pain to God. Consequently, my faith became an essential tool for navigating through this painful process.

I had to cease wrestling, grappling, and resisting God's assistance. Embracing the reality of what had occurred taught me to stop asking "why" and instead relinquish everything to God, allowing Him to guide me toward healing and peace.

I realized that I could not continue fighting on my own. Despite this understanding, I still wondered how I could find peace amidst the raging storm within me. The answer to that was to submit totally to the Lordship of Jesus Christ and to trust the God who is sovereign.

So, in accepting my new reality, I had to learn the belief of "Sanctification." This refers to the concept that occurs when God initiates the divine transformative process of setting us apart. It is where He works within us and through us, to fulfil His purpose of divine service, even during the difficult times of life, thus, bringing about some measure of good in the midst of turbulent and challenging storms.

It was during this time that a change began to take place within me, as God transformed my heart and brought healing. In His own unique way, God ultimately used all the pain for my benefit. Although I may not have fully comprehended how He eventually accomplished it, especially when my heart was still so broken, I had to hold on to faith and trust in God through the process.

During those dark days, my conversations with God would have probably taken on a different tone instead of solely focusing on layer upon layer of sorrow. I now recognize that this repetitive dwelling on sorrow was a maladaptive way of coping with grief for me.

It is easy to build an altar around your pain and almost refuse to let go of it because you feel guilty that perhaps in the process, you might forget your loved one if you choose to be hopeful and start concentrating on living without them. However, it's crucial to understand that moving on takes courage and strength, and there should be no guilt associated with it.

I am learning to express gratitude for the time I had with my mother and the years during which she instilled values that have shaped me into the person I am today. Whenever I miss her, I reflect on how incredibly fortunate I was to have had her in my life. I would not trade those moments for anything. I also acknowledge that her memory is a precious treasure that will endure.

However, I have come to understand that those treasured moments and the person herself were never truly mine to possess but to enjoy momentarily. Although this realization can be painful for someone grieving the loss of a loved one, personally, it has helped me cope with my loss. My mother was simply on loan to me for a limited time. Although I may not have been prepared to let her go, her time on Earth ended abruptly through no fault of my own.

In light of this understanding, it is worth considering what our departed loved ones would expect from us. Instead of dwelling on our grief, our departed loved ones would, in most cases, desire for us to move forward in life and release any feelings of guilt. They would want us to embrace the new reality of living without their physical presence while knowing that they reside within our hearts eternally. It is important to acknowledge that although our loved ones were part of the previous chapter of our lives, the present reality calls for us to turn a new page without their physical presence on the Earth. Despite the pain this may bring, it is perfectly acceptable because life must continue, and it is okay to find the courage to forge ahead.

Most of our loved ones would not want us to mourn them indefinitely. They would encourage us to live fully and not remain trapped in perpetual sorrow. It is often said that the ones left behind find it harder to cope with the loss than those who have passed away. Therefore, we must choose to live a life that would make our loved ones proud, as if they were watching us from heaven, celebrating our accomplishments on Earth.

By honouring their memory through our actions and achievements, we can find a sense of purpose and continue living a life that reflects their influence and love. It is a way to keep their spirit alive while embracing the journey ahead.

CHAPTER 13

A TURN AROUND

It was beginning to feel like a rollercoaster ride of emotions over and over again. By November 1994, I was down again, and this time it was severe. I sank into another deep depression and found myself spending more time in bed, eating poorly, and neglecting my self- care. I had reached a point where life seemed hopeless, and I simply wanted to die. "What is happening now?" I had thought I was over the sadness and grief.

During this challenging period, I vividly remember how God rallied my friends in the choir, particularly those whom I was close to. They took turns to come and be with me, offering their support. Some would provide words of encouragement and pray for me, while others would lend a helping hand by cooking my meals. Some individuals, without uttering any words of condemnation, judgement, or sermons about how

Christians should not experience depression, would simply be there for me.

One special sister, named Grace, became a close friend and a source of immense comfort for me. She was what Christians call a "sister in the Lord" because of our shared faith and connection through the church. Grace was someone I had a deep bond with, and she played a significant role in supporting me during that difficult time. She was truly my saving grace.

Grace came into my life at a very pivotal and yet sensitive time. I recall how she rang me daily and said that she was coming to spend Christmas with me. I told her that I would be fine, but she insisted that she would come anyway. She did not take no for an answer, and before I knew it, she was at my home. She later told me that she had to come because she could not trust me with myself anymore, because I was sinking into a deep and dark place, and she did not like it.

I often smile now when I think of Grace and her genuine love and kindness towards me, because she was truly a Godsend to me during my time of need and despair, and I have come to realize that she was right— because I too could not even trust myself at that point. I am aware that she fervently prayed for my recovery.

Despite my constant repetition of "I want to die," she was the only one brave enough to rebuke me for uttering such negative words. Even to this day, I cannot comprehend how God managed to rescue me from the depths of despair. What I do know is that it was through the prayers of well-intentioned Christian friends who stood by my side during that challenging period. God utilized them as instruments to save me from the destructive mental anguish I was experiencing.

In 1995, I started to navigate my loss by engaging in heartfelt conversations with my Christian friend, Grace, who had been there for me during my darkest moments and selflessly chose to spend her Christmas with a friend struggling with depression.

With Grace by my side, life seemed to gain a glimmer of brightness. She was always there for me, readily available whenever I reached out to her. It felt as if she were a mother hen, fiercely protective and nurturing when it came to my well-being. Her unswerving presence, loyalty, maturity, and unwavering support made me feel an overwhelming sense of love and genuine care.

What intensified the depression I felt and contributed to my poor mental health was the absence of a job and a sense of abandonment. I had been applying for various positions without success. During that time, I was willing to undertake any role in the hospitality industry. Despite knowing it would involve demanding work, I enjoyed working with food and was prepared to dedicate the necessary hours to fund my education. I simply needed to find something that would allow me to resume my studies.

Moreover, with my mother's passing, I was now responsible for paying my own fees and had to work exceptionally hard to survive on whatever salary I could attain. Consequently, I began considering exploring opportunities in a different location. I discussed this with Grace and informed her that I was contemplating leaving England to relocate to South Africa.

One of my aunties was living in South Africa and had invited me to come over for a break, considering all that had happened with the loss of my mother. I confided in my friend Grace about my contemplation of leaving London. I still remember the shock on her face when I broke the news to her. She pleaded, "Please don't go. Life won't be the same without you." As I continued to ponder the decision to leave England, I simultaneously prayed and sought God's guidance.

A few months passed while I was still in the process of making plans when I received some shocking news. My auntie, who had invited me to South Africa, suddenly passed away. The news hit me like a ton of bricks, and I was overcome with shock and devastation.

Once again, I found myself battling with grief and questioning why such a tragedy had occurred. I understood that trials are a part of life and that we can't always find answers to everything, but our human nature always seeks understanding in the face of life's challenges.

As I tried to process the sudden death of my aunt, who had been like a big sister, mother and close friend to me, my mind struggled to comprehend why she, too, had been taken away at such a young age, leaving behind three small children.

I felt troubled and concerned about the future of those kids. It was a difficult time for me, and I knew I was not in a suitable mental state to take care of anyone while I was still grappling with my own grief and loss.

I felt helpless in assisting my auntie's children, even though my heart longed to help. However, without a job and struggling to take care of myself physically and emotionally, I felt incapable of providing any support. It seemed unjust for these innocent children to endure further turmoil, especially after the loss of their parents. I kept questioning myself about how I could help, a question that would linger for years to come.

While my auntie's death was profoundly disturbing and painful, by the time I received the news, I had begun to learn how to process my anguish and pain in healthier, more adaptive ways. I was gradually finding ways to navigate through grief. Living alone allowed me the space to mourn for my auntie in my own personal manner. Although sadly, I remained in denial for a long time, especially not having attended her funeral, to allow for closure.

CHAPTER 14

"YOU HAVE CIRCLED THIS MOUNTAIN LONG"

Those were the words spoken by the Almighty God to Moses as he and the Israelites wandered in the wilderness, circling the same mountain for an extended period. Similarly, I had spent enough time meandering through the hills of sorrow, grief, and pain for far too long. It was now time to shift my focus towards a new direction and claim the land that had been designated for me. I had to take back control of my life.

The Bible itself teaches us about the importance of timing, stating that there is a time and season for every activity under the heavens. It begins with the recognition that there is a time to be born and a time to die. Change was on the horizon, and it was time to embrace it.

As the year was drawing to a close, my dear friend Grace was relieved that I had decided not to leave England hastily. Her unwavering support and encouragement played a significant role in strengthening my relationship with God.

I devoted time to prayer and reading my Bible while engaging in heartfelt conversations with Him throughout the day, as one would with a trusted friend. I discovered that disconnecting from the distractions of the world and finding solace in God's presence brought me a profound sense of peace and clarity.

During those moments of isolation and solitude, a spark of hope ignited within me, and I relearned the art of dreaming. It was in those quiet spaces that I began to envision a brighter future and nurture a renewed sense of hope for what lay ahead.

After an extended period of grieving, I finally started to see glimpses of light in the darkest corners of my life. There was a renewed peace within me that remained unshakable. I couldn't pinpoint the exact moment or the catalyst for this transformation, but I knew that my dear friend Grace played a significant role. She supported me through the most challenging phase of my life and guided me back to God.

Once again, I was learning not to despair, for the joy of the Lord became my strength. It wasn't that God or His joy had ever left my life during the time of my pain, but it felt as though I had rediscovered a long- lost friend and was once again relishing His presence. Each day, my connection with Him grew stronger, and I drew more and more strength from Him. In this new- found intimacy, God began speaking directly to my spirit, revealing specific things, and guiding me along my journey.

I surrendered everything to Him—my pain, my regrets, my weaknesses, my shattered dreams—giving it all to God and making Him the Lord of my life once again. Those were profoundly precious moments for me, and only God truly knew the extensive work He was doing in my life.

I vividly remember a particular day when God revealed a specific date to me: the 7th of September 1996. Instantly, I searched for it on the calendar and discovered that it fell on a Saturday. Initially, I assumed it indicated that one of my friends would be getting married or that something special would soon occur. Little did I know that God was actually revealing the date of my own future wedding.

I also recall a Saturday morning when I went shopping with a dear friend. We ventured to Oxford Street in London and entered a certain department store that no longer exists today. The store happened to be one of my mother's favourite places to shop. At that time, the store offered high-quality clothing at affordable prices.

As I perused the selection of ladies' clothes, my attention was caught by a display of party dresses. Some were in an elegant ivory shade, while others were a soft peach colour. Excitedly, I turned to my friend and shared my intention to purchase seven of those dresses for my bridesmaids. Her reaction was immediate and filled with laughter, causing her to cover her mouth to stifle the sound. "Paula, you must be joking!" she exclaimed incredulously. I smiled and reassured her that I was entirely serious.

I expressed my determination to start by purchasing four of the dresses and return for the remaining three the following week. Perplexed, she responded, "But you're not even in a relationship with anyone!" With confidence, I replied, "I know, but I have a deep conviction that my wedding is approaching soon." Undeterred, I made my way to the cash register and completed the purchase of the four dresses. My friend stood beside me, still in disbelief at my unexpected decision.

Throughout the entire journey back home, she kept chuckling and found the shopping spree very amusing. I couldn't blame her for laughing, as I even chuckled at myself for purchasing dresses without a groom or any idea about who my bridesmaids would be. Since both of us knew that there was no man in my life at the time, I confidently told her to watch and see what the LORD would do in my life.

I am really not sure where that kind of conviction came from because I was so certain that nothing could shake my faith. Well, my friend laughed all the way home because she still couldn't believe what she had just witnessed.

A week later, I went back to the store and purchased three more of the party dresses, bringing the total to seven. I informed my friend that I had returned to the store and bought the remaining dresses. She responded by saying, "Okay, Paula this is really bizarre now; you don't know who your bridesmaids will be or what sizes they will need." I confidently told her that whoever they may be when the time comes for me to get married, they will undoubtedly fit into the dresses. I could not explain the unwavering faith that God had bestowed upon me as He continued to heal my heart. It felt as if I had experienced a rebirth, a new- found sense of purpose. Everything just felt so right and reassuring.

One Sunday afternoon at church, the same pastor who helped me before, whom I held in high regard noticed me and asked me to sit down. She looked at me with intensity and began speaking to me about my life. Her words have stayed with me ever since. She said, "You have grown, and I don't mean it in a natural or physical sense, but spiritually. The work God is doing in you will be enduring. He is intricately stitching your life together, like the art of embroidery. Each stitch is tight, ensuring that nothing unravels. He is perfecting His work in you."

She continued to share a few more things and then tears welled up in her eyes as she proclaimed, "God is about to do something new in your life, and though I don't know the specifics, I can assure you that it will be good."

As we were parting ways, she added, "Paula, please come back and share with me when it happens because whatever it is, it will be great."

I wholeheartedly agreed with her words because I knew deep down that she was truly hearing from God. She was speaking about things that were hidden, mysteries that I had never disclosed to anyone. They were discussions I had held with God in the secret place of my heart. I recognized it as the handiwork of God because she was unveiling and affirming those private conversations, confirming the things I had been discussing with God about my life during moments of prayer. It was an incredibly surreal experience.

Leaving the church that day, I felt an overwhelming sense of joy and peace; my faith was invigorated. It was as if my life were taking a new path, and I was embracing the transformed and renewed version of myself.

The darkness that had overshadowed me in the storms of life was fading into the past. I now had the courage to believe again, to truly live and hope once more. Slowly but surely, I was rediscovering meaning in my life.

CHAPTER 15

A NEW CHAPTER

A few months later, a male friend of two years, whom I had met through the choir, started giving me a ride home after our rehearsals. As it turned out, we lived in the same neighbourhood. Later on, I discovered from our mutual choir friends, including my dear friend Grace, that they had been subtly trying to bring us together, believing that we would make a good couple.

However, at that time, I had no interest in pursuing a relationship with that particular male friend. My attention had shifted towards another young man in the choir. Unfortunately, I was oblivious to the fact that the person I would eventually marry was right before my eyes, always keen to offer a lift home after each rehearsal.

In due course, a remarkable event occurred one night as I knelt beside my bed in prayer. It was my usual routine, offering my general thanksgiving prayers and surrendering everything to God as I did every day. I distinctly remember uttering the words, "God, even if I never marry, I will continue to love and serve You until my last breath. LORD you are my life." As I concluded my prayer, something extraordinary happened.

I heard God's voice in a way I had never experienced before—it was as clear and real as if someone had called my name. The room was illuminated, and I was alone in the house, leaving no doubt that I had indeed heard a distinct voice. I was unaware of the source, so I instinctively scanned the room in the direction from which I perceived the sound. I knew without a doubt that God had spoken to me, confirming that I would get married and the person I was meant to marry.

Curiosity got the better of me, and I asked once more, but this time, there was silence. God had spoken once, and He knew that I had heard His message loud and clear. The decision was left to me—to proceed or not.

That night, I could not sleep due to an overwhelming excitement, not only because of what was revealed to me, but primarily because I had audibly heard the voice of God. It was an experience beyond belief that He had chosen to communicate with me in such a direct manner.

Since that day, I have never heard His voice audibly again. Instead, His guidance reaches me through my spirit-intuition, His word, people, and various life situations and circumstances where I discern His voice.

The next day, my intuition led me to the calendar, and my eyes landed on the date I had circled the previous year: September 7th. That was the day I believed one of my friends would be getting married, not considering myself in the equation. However, as I started piecing the puzzle together, it became clear that God had been preparing me for the man He had in mind for me to marry.

Although I had initially denied my feelings towards this man in prayer, viewing him only as a good friend who would do anything for me, I realized it was a God- ordained situation.

The subsequent days unfolded in a way that made me truly believe that God has the power to transform one's heart and mind, swiftly persuading them to love someone. The scales fell from my eyes, revealing the truth of what had been happening all along. I cannot even explain how love entered my heart, but I found myself head over heels in love overnight, like a smitten schoolgirl. It was yet another miracle.

I recall my choir sisters' commenting, "We've been watching you and wondering how long it would take for you two to become a couple." I continuously insisted that I had no idea and that he was merely my friend. However, that young man eventually pursued me and asked for my hand in marriage. The details of how we met and our journey to marriage are recounted in another book.

As my now husband and I continued to get to know each other better, I noticed that many of the things I had sought guidance from God about were being confirmed. It became undeniably clear that this relationship was a result of God's plan.

Right from the beginning, we prioritized honesty and transparency, which allowed our friendship to blossom into a deeper and more meaningful connection. Within a few months, our dynamics shifted from being brother and sister in Christ to becoming future husband and wife.

One day, in a moment that felt both surprising and surreal, my soon-to-be husband got down on one knee and proposed to me. It was remarkable because even the details of the proposal aligned with what God had revealed to me in the past. He had spoken to me about the moments leading to this time years before, and His words were reaffirmed at that special moment. To summarize the rest of the story, we got married on September 7th, 1996—the exact date God had given me one year earlier.

My wedding day arrived, and it was a joyous occasion filled with celebration and the unexpected support of many generous individuals. One particular surprise came in the form of a woman I had not previously known but met at a friend's bridal shower in London.

This lady, who had apparently known my mother well during her time as a manager, introduced herself as a former junior colleague from the airline where my mother had worked. In a heartfelt manner, she expressed her deep admiration for my mother, recounting how she had assumed a maternal role in her life. Notably, my mother made significant contributions in terms of guidance, training, and invaluable assistance during this woman's tenure as junior cabin crew member. In gratitude for all the help my mother had provided, she had pledged to do anything she could to contribute towards my wedding day.

This encounter reminded me of the countless instances when my mother would take the time to greet people from all walks of life and teach us the importance of kindness, regardless of someone's social status—a virtue she constantly emphasized.

On my wedding day, I was taken aback by the fact that I did not feel a sense of grief for my mother, nor did I shed a single tear. Instead, I was overwhelmed with an immense amount of love from family and friends who had contributed to the organization of my wedding. I was especially touched by the warm reception I received from my husband's family, who embraced me wholeheartedly as a new member of their family.

My mother-in-law referred to me as her daughter and assured me that she would now assume the role of my mother, fully aware of the loss of my own mother. Again, this was an answer to my prayers, to be married into a loving family.

I felt a new-found strength within me and a resilience in coping with my loss. Although I had come to terms with the fact that my mother was no longer physically present, I could not help but wish she could have been there to share in the joy of my wedding day. The pain had subsided over time, and a profound healing had occurred within me.

Throughout the wedding planning process, memories of my mother's final visit to me in London flooded my mind. I remembered how she had sat with me as we meticulously crafted the guest list and how we had excitedly ventured to the stationery shop together. Her words echoed in my ears, as she had continuously expressed her belief that I would marry soon and encouraged us to plan accordingly.

I also recalled my mother's desire for her children to marry after the age of 25 and not younger. As mentioned earlier, she believed it was crucial to fully understand oneself and possibly explore the world through travelling, especially during one's single life, before settling into marriage. It struck me how the things my mother had spoken and wished for during her time on Earth had come to pass. Her words held a special significance, serving as a poignant reminder of her presence in my life, even in her physical absence.

While I miss her daily, nowadays when I cry, it is usually tears of gratitude to God for giving me a good mother like her. I often think of others who have never known the love of a parent, so I feel blessed to have experienced the love of a mother. I never knew my father; as mentioned earlier, he passed away when I was a baby, so my mother played the roles of both mum and dad.

CHAPTER 16

BITTER-SWEET MOMENTS

The year before I got married, I had a disturbing dream that I had given birth to a stillborn baby. In the dream, the doctors said something was wrong with the baby. I woke up from that dream thinking, "No, it cannot happen to me." I had come to know that God spoke to me through dreams and visions, but I decided to dismiss and ignore this dream without much thought and neglected to pray seriously about it.

The first year of marriage was a time for us to truly get to know each other. I have often heard many people say that the first year of marriage is usually the most challenging, but for us, it was quite the opposite. It was a good year. Surprisingly, the following year turned out even better as we were blessed with our first baby girl, followed by another girl three years later.

Pregnancy went smoothly for both of our girls, but labour and delivery were quite difficult. Despite the challenges, our joy knew no bounds upon welcoming our daughters into the world.

Another three years later, we were once again blessed with another pregnancy. Just like with our previous babies, we wanted to keep the gender a surprise until the baby was born. So, we made the decision to wait. At 12 weeks, we went for our first ultrasound scan, and just like before, we were filled with excitement to see how our baby was developing.

In the scan room, the technician carefully scanned and checked all the body parts, confirming what she could see. As I continued observing the technician's facial expressions, I noticed a change in her look, and a puzzled expression appeared on her face. She informed us that she had seen something that appeared to be a sign of an abnormality, but she needed to consult with the specialist and confirm her findings. We were then asked to wait within the hospital grounds and return in an hour to meet with the consultant.

Overwhelmed with worry and anxiety about the unknown, my husband and I found a quiet spot outside the hospital. We held hands and prayed, entrusting everything we didn't understand to God.

When we returned to the scan room, the consultant took a closer look at the baby in my womb. He confirmed that he, too, noticed a fluid-like substance suggesting a sign of abnormality around the neck area, indicating the need to carry out further tests to be certain. One of the tests involved taking a sample of the amniotic fluid from the embryo sac to examine it for any abnormalities, but this procedure carried the risk of miscarriage.

The consultant then presented us with another shocking option, which was to consider terminating the pregnancy should the baby have any chromosome abnormality. It was a difficult moment as he suggested the possibility of ending the life of our innocent child. Both my husband and I were horrified to even hear the word 'termination' as an option. The consultant further added that in certain circumstances some people choose this option because they don't want their child to be born and suffer. In response, we told him that, as Christians, it was not even a consideration for us.

Regardless of whether our baby was born with a disability, we believed that they were a gift from God and that they belonged to Him but given to us to nurture. The doctor said the decision was ours, and if we returned at 24 weeks, he would re-evaluate the findings.

Leaving the consultant's office, I felt relieved to depart from all the distressing news. My husband and I decided not to go for any more scans as they were too distressing. Instead, we would wait until the delivery and go directly to the hospital.

As time passed, I reached 35 weeks in my pregnancy, and the baby remained active. I spoke words of love and welcome to him or her, affirming their presence.

I remember being summoned for jury service during that time; due to my condition, I was reluctant to participate. Being heavily pregnant made me easily tired as I tried to fulfil my duties as a wife and mother, which was no easy task.

So, I decided to call the court and inquire if there was any possibility of being excused. They informed me that I should try to attend at least one court session and assured me they would cover my travel expenses. However, it was not the travel expenses that concerned me, but rather the need for rest. The thought of commuting back and forth on public transport while leaving my younger daughter with a caregiver was unappealing.

Despite my reservations, I recognized the obligation to fulfil my civic duty, so I reluctantly attended jury duty as required by the law. During our lunch break, I found myself seated with a woman who shared her heartbreaking story of losing her baby and the immense pain she endured. I listened to her account with profound empathy, although I could not fully grasp the depth of her loss. After lunch, we reconvened for one final court session before being dismissed following the verdict.

On my way home, my mind was preoccupied with the woman's heartbreaking story of miscarriage that I had heard at the courthouse. Upon arriving home, it was a joy to be reunited with my daughters, as I had asked one of my nieces to watch over them for the day. However, later that day, a thought struck me: "I haven't felt my baby move today." I shared this concern with my niece, half-jokingly suggesting that perhaps the baby was tired of the courtroom drama and decided to sleep.

After my niece left, my husband returned from work, and as we all prepared for bed, I could not shake off the worry that something was amiss. Throughout the day and into the night, the baby had remained still, unresponsive to my attempts to nudge or speak to him or her. It was then that I confided in my husband, expressing my growing apprehension about the lack of movement of our baby.

I made a phone call to the hospital, and they advised me to come in immediately. Leaving our daughters in the care of my sister, my husband and I drove swiftly to the hospital. When we arrived, we were directed to a side ward and shown into a room where we were informed that the consultant would conduct a scan soon. Shortly thereafter, the consultant entered the room and inquired about any foetal movements I had felt throughout the day. I expressed that I hadn't felt any movements at all.

At that moment, I felt a wave of apprehension wash over me. Hospitals have always carried a sense of foreboding for me, as they often herald bad news. And in my experience, anything negative leaves a bitter taste, which is never pleasant.

As the doctor scanned my tummy, a faint heartbeat reached my ears, but she clarified that it was my own heartbeat, not the baby's. The screen displaying the scan was angled away from me, obscuring my view, but I carefully observed the expressions on the doctor's face. Confusion seemed to be etched across her features. Despite her professionalism, her changing countenance hinted at an issue. Yet, she persisted in her attempts to locate the baby's heartbeat, as if unwilling to accept the possibility of its absence. When she eventually set down the handheld monitor, I instinctively knew what she was about to convey.

Like Job in the Bible, who lamented, "What I feared has come upon me," I felt the weight of the dreaded news crashing down. The doctor's words were barely uttered before I found myself screaming, exclaiming a vehement "No!" In that moment, she and the nurse discreetly left my husband and me alone in the room, granting us the solitude to confront the outcome.

Amidst the cacophony of my cries and tears, a sense of shock engulfed me, distinct from any previous experience, for this time it was my own child who had ceased to exist within me. I felt trapped, devoid of escape. Whom could I turn to? What actions should I take? My mind churned with questions, but there was no solace, no respite, only an overwhelming turmoil.

After a few agonizing minutes, the doctor returned to the room, accompanied by the nurse. I glanced at both the doctor and nurse attending to me, noticing their tear-streaked faces. It was a rare occurrence for them and an unusual sight, one that deeply shocked me and broke my heart.

The doctor gently held my hand, offering sincere condolences to my husband and me, speaking softly as she explained what needed to be done. She requested that I return in three days to deliver the baby.

After returning home, we broke the news to our two daughters, who struggled to comprehend how the baby could have passed away while still in mummy's womb. We chose to share the news only with immediate family members, but by the following day, visitors began arriving at our home to pay their respects.

However, I had no desire to see anyone or be comforted with empty words, similar to when I lost my mother. The pain I was experiencing demanded solitude to process the devastating reality.

CHAPTER 17

THE UNEXPECTED

Usually, people may find it challenging to truly understand and relate to a tragedy unless they have personally experienced something similar. While they may listen attentively and offer empathy, the depth of your pain may be difficult for them to fully grasp because every individual's experience is unique. Even though the experience may bring about a new- found understanding, it's unlikely that others can fully feel the anguish of another person.

I am someone who excels at connecting with others on an individual level. However, I have found that the advice or counsel I received in the past has occasionally exacerbated my wounds rather than providing solace or support.

I vividly remember a cousin who during my loss said to me, "Don't worry, you're not the first one to have a miscarriage." Those words struck me with horror and disbelief. In that moment, I wanted to lash out at her and demand that she leaves my room. However, I realized that she didn't fully grasp the weight of her statement. So, I chose to forgive her, letting go of my anger and disappointment.

Although I felt the urge to shout, "Leave me alone, all of you! This isn't just a miscarriage; it's something different." My baby, had he or she been born, would have survived because he or she was already in the last trimester and 35 weeks old. The loss I experienced was indescribable and beyond words. I remained numb for a long time.

After three days, we returned to the hospital for the delivery. Once again, it was a night-time admission when we arrived, and the hospital staff provided me with a private room in the labour ward. Regardless of life or death, we had made the conscious choice not to know our baby's gender beforehand. Just like with our other two children, we wanted the gender to be revealed at the moment of birth. We had always chosen not to know the gender of any of our babies, as we believed the surprise of discovering it at birth was truly worth the anticipation.

Soon after admission, labour was induced, and I was making steady progress. In the early hours of the morning, my waters broke, marking the beginning of a physically and emotionally excruciating labour. Through intense physical pain, I delivered our third baby. She was a girl! Our baby arrived on the morning of January 29th in the year 2003, at 9:20 am. She was immediately wrapped up while I underwent the necessary cleaning procedures.

After the birth of our baby, she was presented to us, and at that moment, we held our baby girl for the first time. I clearly remember the moment when I first laid eyes on her. Embracing my daughter with tears streaming down my face as I spoke to her softly, "You should have let me see your eyes," I whispered, questioning why she had chosen to leave us.

In my delivery situation, the midwife informed me that pushing would require extra effort since the baby was no longer alive. The midwife further explained that the body did not differentiate between a living or deceased baby—it simply recognized the presence of a baby that needed to be birthed. Although distressed, I found that aspect truly fascinating.

The pain of labour and delivery coupled with emotional grief were overwhelming, and I could not help but think that this level of suffering should never be endured by any woman. It was an experience that I would not wish upon anyone.

After delivery, I lay in that hospital bed, watching my husband cuddle our daughter with tears in his eyes and a heavy heart, the task of putting my emotions into words felt unbearable. Was this truly happening to us? The pain was too overwhelming to comprehend. I struggled to hold her for too long, consumed by heartbreak and overwhelmed by shock.

Countless questions raced through my mind, desperate for answers: Why was my baby born asleep? Can anyone explain that to me? Did I somehow cause this tragedy? How could I have done anything to harm a baby I loved so deeply? Was it possible that I had physically exerted myself? Was stress a factor? Did I receive sufficient support from my husband during my pregnancy? Who can unravel this mystery?

Despite the challenges of that day, I could not help but gaze upon our daughter's exquisite beauty and pondered over the person she would have grown up to be and who she would resemble. We cherished those precious few minutes with her before she was gently taken away from our embrace.

I may not have been prepared to let her go, but her time on Earth ended abruptly through no fault of my own. I was overwhelmed with confusion and had no desire to engage in conversation with anyone. Later that morning, compassionate medical personnel approached our ward and sensitively discussed the next steps following the loss of a baby.

They kindly offered the services of a counsellor who could speak with me. However, I was in such a fragile state that I could not fathom discussing the traumatic experience with anyone, not even with my husband, who was there throughout the experience. The counsellor empathetically asked if I would like to speak at a later time, but I declined, feeling incapable of opening my heart to a stranger. She provided me with some information in case I changed my mind and wished to seek support in the future. I expressed gratitude for her consideration, but in that moment of profound grief, I simply longed to be left alone.

Amidst my sorrow, I couldn't help but question why God had bestowed this precious life upon us, only to take her away before I could even catch a glimpse of her eyes and share an intimate connection. Once again, I found myself yearning for someone to provide answers about what had happened to my baby.

The doctors claimed it was an occurrence that defied medical explanation, something that simply happens to a small number of women. I had now become one of those statistical mothers who had experienced the devastation of a stillbirth. Although that fact held little significance and didn't matter to me, my quest for answers turned towards a higher power – God.

Until now, I had never questioned God about His actions or lack thereof, as I understood that He was the Almighty, and some mysteries belonged solely to Him. Yet, in this instance, I couldn't help but wonder why my precious child's life was abruptly cut so short. Eventually, my questioning shifted to understanding the purpose of her brief existence, which only added to my confusion.

Despite the fact that this was another one of the most difficult experiences I had ever faced, I sought to find meaning within my limited human capacity, attempting to cope with yet another tragic loss. I loved my baby unconditionally, even before I had the chance to know her.

I suppose there are numerous things that I may never comprehend or fully grasp. It is inherent in human nature to question and seek explanations for the events that unfold around us.

We found ourselves spending yet another day in the hospital, diligently attending to the necessary paperwork, arrangements for a postmortem and her funeral. Our intention was to ensure a respectful and organized farewell, returning her to the embrace of God the Father, her Maker.

Throughout this emotionally challenging process, the staff at St. Thomas's Hospital in London displayed remarkable sensitivity and care, tending to our needs with unwavering professionalism.

As we left the hospital empty-handed on a cold, snowy winter morning, we departed with heavy hearts, filled with sorrow at the thought of leaving our baby in the hospital mortuary. The mere mention of the word 'mortuary' took me years to utter, as it sent shudders down my spine, evoking the image of a loved one confined within a refrigerator.

The hospital staff were exceptionally competent and professional in their interactions with me. Upon discharge, they guided my husband and me through a discreet back door, ensuring that I would not encounter other mothers or witness the sights and sounds of babies in the regular ward.

I was deeply appreciative of their compassionate understanding of our grief. While leaving our baby behind was devastating, the anguish of returning home without her was equally excruciating. It signified that I was about to face a test I had never anticipated. The cold, snowy winter day only compounded my feelings of distress, making the day of discharge even more dreadful.

Once we arrived back home, I sought solace in solitude for a while before retrieving our daughters from my sister's house. Although I anticipated that our girls would have questions upon seeing their father and expressing their desire to meet their sister, it was an incredibly challenging situation for me, as I was still profoundly shaken by the entire ordeal. I needed to gather strength and come up with an appropriate explanation tailored to their age when they returned home.

Therefore, while in the hospital, I had requested of my husband to allow them to see their sister. However, he believed they were still too young to fully understand the magnitude of what had occurred.

So, when the girls returned home that day, we prepared ourselves as best we could and chose our words carefully to explain to a 5-year-old and a 3-year- old what happened to the baby in mummy's tummy. My oldest daughter asked if she could go and see her sister, but her dad gently declined.

Although I still felt she should have been allowed to at the time, I am now grateful for my husband's judgement in suggesting that it was not a good idea. This is because, when my father-in-law passed away many years later, our girls were allowed to see him in a coffin, and to this day, my older daughter says she wishes she hadn't seen him like that. It was traumatic for her to see him lifeless after knowing him as the loving granddad whom she had spent time with while he was alive.

The days that followed were incredibly challenging as we waited for the post-mortem investigation to be conducted and awaited the subsequent results. The mourning period was especially difficult as we prepared for her funeral.

Our pastor visited our home to discuss the funeral program. We had named our little girl 'Sepo,' which means 'Hope' in my mother tongue, Silozi, from the Western Province of Zambia.

As a result, we finally laid our baby to rest almost two weeks after her passing because we had requested a post-mortem examination to determine the cause of death, as mentioned earlier.

Although we had been told that there was a sign of a chromosome abnormality discovered, the investigations yielded no answers to ascertain a definite cause of death, leaving me still questioning God for an explanation.

CHAPTER 18

SEPO, MY DAUGHTER

What I will never forget is the pain that overwhelmed me on the day of Sepo's funeral. I remember telling my husband that I could not bear it, as it brought back vivid memories of my mother's burial. All I wanted was to escape, to have someone stand in for me while I remained at home, weeping in solitude.

However, this was something I knew demanded my presence and I would have to go through it, no matter how broken I felt. Sometimes when faced with challenges beyond our ability to cope, we think we are unable to handle tragedy but somehow, from an unknown source, strength and courage rise within us. I found myself mustering the resolve to attend the funeral of my own baby. In that moment of darkness, my husband emerged as a pillar of unwavering support, a channel through which God's strength manifested.

As we stood outside the chapel, I observed a small coffin being brought in a beautiful hearse, accompanied by a well-dressed and professional gentleman. Despite never having the chance to meet anyone in this world, Sepo was treated with utmost respect. It was a solemn sight. A notable moment was witnessing my husband who had expressed the wish to serve as the Pall bearer. The sight of my husband carrying our daughter's tiny casket evoked a profound sense of distress.

In retrospect, no other person was more suited to facilitate the return of our daughter back into our heavenly Father's embrace than her biological and earthly father.

Bishop Delroy Powell, not only our pastor at the time, but also a close friend of my husband's family, conducted the ceremony with such grace and empathy. His words were a balm to our grieving souls. Following a brief church service, we proceeded to lay Sepo to rest in a nearby cemetery with immediate family and close friends in attendance.

The journey back home from the cemetery proved to be an agonizing one. The realization that we had left our precious Sepo behind in that silent place felt deeply unsettling. However, amidst the anguish, I had to find solace in the belief that she was at peace, embraced by the presence of her Creator.

Though I may never comprehend the full scope of the life experiences I've endured or their purpose, I have come to recognize moments when God graciously provides warnings about His plans or even alerts us to the malevolent intentions of the devil.

I sometimes reflect on the dream I had in 1996, long before our baby was conceived. I have often pondered whether that dream served as a warning, necessitating spiritual intervention to thwart any plans the enemy might have had, and whether I missed that opportunity. Alternatively, could it have been a glimpse into the future, similar to the visions God has bestowed upon me in the past?

I reflect on the days before my mother passed away, when I had a dream about one of my mother's siblings' dying. It made me realize the importance of paying attention to my dreams, as they seemed to be a form of spiritual communication that God intended for me to heed.

This also led me to recall the encounter with a lady at the courthouse during my jury service. The day she had shared her story of miscarriage coincided with the tragic loss of my own baby inside my womb. Unbeknownst to me at the time, the events unfolding from that discussion would mirror my own experience, culminating in the heart-breaking loss of my baby.

In hindsight, I wondered if the lady at the courthouse were an angel sent to prepare me for the impending tragedy that awaited me that very night when my baby was pronounced dead in my womb.

So many questions, guesses, and assumptions arose within me. For many of these, I may never truly know why things unfolded as they did. However, I am learning to make peace with the various events in my life and find purpose in my pain. The realization that God communicates through multiple avenues has become a significant source of assurance for my faith in Him.

I am learning to share my story, hoping that as you read this book, you will come to understand that life encompasses both unexpected twists and turns as well as delightful moments that bring immense joy. Just as the sun faithfully shines each day, we can be equally confident that God is always prepared to accompany us through life's darkest paths, holding our hand as we navigate the valleys. Even in the bleakest moments, there remains a glimmer of hope and the potential for triumph.

Each individual is faced with the choice of either dwelling in trauma or embarking on a journey of healing and wholeness. While there may be more sorrows to come, I have chosen the path of healing, and my aim is to inspire others to believe that they can live a fulfilling life, even in the aftermath of a shattered heart burdened by grief.

A year later, God blessed us once again with the gift of a fourth child. Our first son. However, prior to this, I had experienced a disturbing dream where I heard a menacing voice proclaim, "This one will die too." Alarmed, I woke my husband and shared the dream with him. Without hesitation, he urged us to pray. Together, we stood steadfast in prayer, rebuking the devil and his deceitful tactics. Though he attempted to sow fear within us through scaremongering, we were well aware of his schemes and refused to succumb.

During that same year, I received the heart- wrenching news of my grandmother's passing. It was a deeply sorrowful time for me, made more difficult by the fact that I could not travel to Zambia due to my pregnancy. Therefore, I had to mourn from a distance, feeling the weight of grief from afar.

It was incredibly difficult because my grandmother had played a significant role in raising us alongside my mother. She was like a second mother to us, and during our formative years, she had been one of the primary caregivers we knew.

Given the circumstances, I could not afford to succumb to grief once more, especially while carrying a child. It wouldn't be fair to the baby. We bid our final farewell to my grandmother, and despite the profound loss, life continued to move forward.

The subsequent months proved to be relatively smooth as my pregnancy progressed without any major complications. Despite carrying out my household responsibilities and ensuring that my daughters were dropped off at school, I managed to handle everything with relative ease. However, the birth of our son was a prolonged and excruciating labour experience.

It struck me as peculiar that while my pregnancies themselves were generally uneventful, the labour and delivery processes consistently posed significant challenges and caused great concern, often necessitating emergency Caesarean section deliveries. That is, except for my beloved, Sepo, who came into the world through a vaginal birth. Following the arrival of our fourth child, our first son, we were incredibly fortunate to welcome yet another baby boy into our lives another two years later.

I am grateful to God for the five children He has given us. While we are entrusted with the stewardship of our four living children, we also include Sepo in our family equation, even though she is now embraced by our heavenly Father in eternity. She is still very much a part of our family.

Our journey has not always been easy, but we could not have made it this far without God's guidance and support.

Reflecting on the ups and downs, I realize that my life holds great value, even during those moments when I felt like giving up after my mother's passing. I would not trade this path for anything else, as I genuinely cherish my role as a wife, mother, and homemaker.

CHAPTER 19

RUN – THE RACE OF LIFE

As I reflect on life today, with each passing year, I am continually amazed at how short our earthly existence truly is. The apostle Paul, in the Bible, aptly compares life to a race, and his words resonate deeply. In this world, we are all bestowed with the precious gifts called "life and time." For most of us, we are granted with at least one opportunity to embrace them fully, of course, unless one has encountered the extraordinary circumstance of death and subsequent resurrection, as depicted in certain stories I have come across. It is as if a whistle blows at the very moment of our birth, when time starts with the clock ticking, and the race of life begins in earnest.

The race commences without granting us much choice, from the very moment of our birth until our final breath. Our parents or guardians play a crucial role in aiding our preparation for this race. However, the manner in which we navigate this race ultimately rests upon our own shoulders and the choices we make along the way.

The Bible says, "The race is not always won by the swift, nor the battle by the strong, neither is bread given to the wise, nor riches to men of understanding, nor favour to men of skill; but time and chance happen to them all."

We are all called to run the race to the end and finish well. In the journey of life, it does not matter whether you come first, second, or third; what truly matters is that you run the race, finish strong, and make a significant and productive impact.

The beginning of most races is often smooth; the runners appear fresh, filled with new energy, and confident in their respective lanes. However, just like in the race of life, some individuals may encounter opportunities that make their journey easier, while others may not be as fortunate.

The unifying truth is that "there is a time and a season for every activity under heaven." We all experience birth, and we all face mortality, which makes the race of life a precious gift.

Life itself is bestowed upon us as a gift, but how we choose to utilize it is entirely our own decision. As you navigate your personal race, you will inevitably encounter various obstacles along the way. The initial stages may have seemed effortless, but the middle phases of the race can prove challenging as you reflect on past mistakes and missed opportunities.

The race of life requires patience and endurance. Many people start strong but get derailed by one thing or another. Although the duration of everyone's race varies, they all require speed, effort, and determination. Finishing strong does not mean finishing without scars or perfectly. Therefore, to finish strong and well, one must be willing to hold fast to the end.

In order to finish strong, it is essential for us to determine whether we will react or respond to the challenges life presents. These two choices yield different outcomes: Reacting involves acting in opposition to something, whereas responding entails acting in a positive or favourable manner. While responding brings satisfaction, reacting often triggers an immediate chemical reaction that can sometimes be unfavourable.

The race requires that you run without compromising on the rules, regardless of your pace. The race of life begins at birth and ends at death, but eternal life in Jesus Christ is forever if you are a believer in God.

In a typical athletic race, when the whistle blows, the race begins. One unique aspect of every race is that no two runners have the same number or lane, especially in long-distance races.

Your own distinct number gives you an identity by which you will be recognized in life. As individuals, we are all unique and special people in our own right. Fundamentally, your date of birth, encompassing both the specific day and time of your arrival, serves as a profound symbol of your unique inception into the vast tapestry of existence, irrespective of the number of individuals who may share that particular birth date. There is no one quite like you, and nobody else possesses your unique features nor your fingerprints. Your number is exclusive to you, as is your lane.

While you may appear similar to other runners in terms of appearance and attire, your rhythm and stride are distinct. The race's rules dictate that you remain in your designated lane; regardless of your pace, it is essential to exhibit discipline by staying in your own lane until the race concludes.

Focus is a crucial requirement for the race. It is important to avoid being distracted by the actions of fellow runners. Maintain your focus and refrain from looking backward or sideways to observe who is running alongside you and at what speed they are moving. Instead, concentrate solely on your own race, speed, and pace, without comparing yourself to others.

Just like a woman in labour, there is no competition as to who delivers faster than the other. The end goal is to deliver safely. Therefore, endure the pain in your muscles and push yourself to your maximum, even when the race becomes intense, and it appears that other runners are surpassing you.

Keep your gaze fixed on the finish line and maintain your course. It is possible that you were leading at the beginning of the race but gradually slowed down. The pace at which you initially ran seemed promising, as you were filled with energy and had high hopes of winning. The enthusiasm and vigour with which you started the race may have been remarkable, posing a threat to other runners and igniting contagious excitement. If you can sustain that pace and intensity, nothing can hinder your progress, and no one can overpower you.

However, as you continue to survey the other runners, you may notice a decline in your speed. This sudden deceleration instils a sense of doubt, casting uncertainty upon your ability to finish the race as strongly as you started. Fatigue may begin to settle in, exacerbated by the sight of fellow runners' effortlessly overtaking you. Your vision becomes obscured, dimming the once-clear path ahead. Your muscles protest, screaming with exhaustion, as doubts echo louder in your mind. "I don't think I can make it," you mutter to yourself, acknowledging your weariness.

As these thoughts burden your mind, your focus wavers, and you begin to question your strength and capability to conquer this monumental task. Your heart pounds forcefully within your chest, urging you to push harder. Your muscles strain even more, your heart rate escalates, and a sense of breathlessness results.

Deep within your heart, an unwavering desire to cross the finish line resonates. You acknowledge that even if you were to collapse upon reaching the end, your determination compels you to see this endeavour through. You condition yourself to run your race to the end regardless of what number you are.

Quitting is not, and will never be, an option that you allow yourself to entertain in the race of life.

CHAPTER 20

FINISH WELL, FINISH STRONG

Despondency may set in when you start comparing yourself to other runners. There will always be those who appear faster than you and those who achieve success later in life. When you find yourself being surpassed by many runners, remember that if you remain committed to the two fundamental principles in life's race—patience and perseverance—you will eventually reach the finish line, even if it's not at the same time as others.

The Bible records an account of Lot's family fleeing from an impending calamity that was about to befall their city. As they were leaving, Lot's wife, upon looking back and reflecting on the past, was transformed into a pillar of salt.

Looking back will only serve to delay or halt your progress and intensify feelings of fear, anxiety, and discouragement. The crucial aspect is to finish the race strongly whatever your pace.

When you redirect your thoughts away from competition, comparison, and envy, you create space for personal growth, renewed concentration, and a steadfast commitment to your own journey without being influenced by others.

By undergoing a significant shift in mindset, you choose to discard the cloak of doubt and failure, embracing instead thoughts of resilience and victory.

A brief moment of renewing your mind can work wonders in restoring your confidence and stamina. Your attitude undergoes a sudden shift, and your focus turns towards what truly matters—yourself and the race laid out before you. Remember that even if others have already accomplished their goals, visions, and dreams, it is not too late for you as long as you still possess the gift of life.

Encourage and motivate yourself with thoughts such as "I am nearly there, and I will reach the finish line," recognizing that completing the race is essential for personal growth and maintaining a healthy perspective on things.

Realign yourself and cultivate a mindset that believes in the limitless possibilities that exist with God. Hold on to this reality and truth. While you may admire others, remind yourself that your own path is unique to you and has been specifically designed for you. It cannot and should not be compared to anyone else's journey. The focus should be on finishing well and finishing strong.

In any race, maintaining your stride and staying focused on the ultimate goal is paramount, regardless of the muscle pain or spasms you may experience. You will sweat, pant, grow tired, and thirst, desperately hoping that the remaining strength within you will be sufficient to carry you across the finish line.

Along the way, you will learn that the race of life is filled with obstacles and hardships that befall everyone. However, the rewards and victories that await at the end of a long and challenging race are even greater.

However, some may quit along the way because the existence of the finishing line seems too far- fetched, while others may continue to run at a very slow pace because discouragement has set in due to unfulfilled desires in life's journey.

In the heavenly race, it matters not what number we are; in God's eyes, He has rewards and medals based on finishing well without wavering. When it feels like life's race is too long and tiresome, remember that even if you have been running tirelessly without seeing the finishing line, there is still hope because every race has a start and a finish at some point.

God is your referee and is constantly cheering you on, saying 'you can do it' regardless of how tired you may feel. God is able to renew the pages of your running record, no matter how many races you have run and not won.

God has promised a crown of glory to those who love Him and follow Him. When life's race feels unbearable, He will give you fresh hope and a different perspective, renewed strength, and faith to believe that you can make it to the end. When you drink from the water He provides, your thirst will be quenched; no matter how weary you become, you can come to Him for rest.

Look ahead at what lies before you and avoid dwelling on the past or comparing yourself to others. Make wise decisions in life's race, rejoice in hope, be patient in tribulation, and through faith, have the assurance that your hope in God can carry you to the finish line.

Consider this perspective: When you board a plane as a passenger, you have a clear destination in mind. Whether you travel in first class or economy class becomes irrelevant because all passengers are aware of their destination and duration of the journey, including the associated risks. Each passenger is allocated a specific seat number that is unique to them. No two people share the same seat number since it was assigned to you at the time of booking. If you fail to claim your seat, the plane will still depart without you, and your seat will remain unoccupied. In such cases, other passengers on board may request to occupy any vacant seat if the plane has available space.

As a passenger I have often witnessed a plane appearing fully booked upon making a reservation, only to realize in certain instances as the plane begins to move, that several seats remained unoccupied.

Throughout the entire duration of the flight, no one may have claimed those empty seats. This observation parallels the notion that in life, no one can replace your individual space and existence. Just like when boarding a plane, each person holds a unique boarding pass with a designated seat number and identity.

Therefore, while we may be on the same flight, we do not share our seats with others. Furthermore, our destinations vary from passenger to passenger. Some may be in transit, while others are destined for the flight's final stop.

CHAPTER 21

VANISHED WITHOUT A TRACE

I was reflecting on the profound emotions that Mary must have experienced when she witnessed her sinless son, Jesus Christ, as He was hanging on the cross and enduring a death meant for criminals. Jesus willingly sacrificed Himself for humanity that was undeserving of such love and selflessness. The sacrificial nature of his death never fails to astonish me. Scholars often date the crucifixion of Jesus to approximately when He was 33 years old.

Ruminating on the relatively short time Jesus spent on Earth before his death, I am struck by how young He was. However, the incredible news is that Jesus rose from the dead and continues to live even today. It is worth considering that if it had been God's will, Jesus might have lived a longer life, quite possibly reaching an age as remarkable as 120 years, similar to the Biblical account of Moses in the Old Testament.

As I contemplated this thought, I heard the voice of God in my spirit, affirming that "Jesus died after fulfilling His purpose on Earth." This truth resonated deeply with me, for Jesus Himself stated in the Bible verse of John 17:4, "I have glorified you on the Earth; I have accomplished, {finished, and completed} the work which You have given me to do." Jesus did not depart from Earth leaving His mission unfinished or without a trace. He left having brought glory to God the Father on Earth.

Jesus Christ remains the greatest teacher to have ever graced our planet. His teachings, laws, and principles continue to resonate with believers and non-believers alike. The efficacy of His teachings stems from their inherent power, which becomes evident when applied by anyone who believes in them. These timeless principles endure today; however, it is important to note that belief in Jesus Christ and knowing Him personally hold greater significance than merely practicing His teachings alone, as some tend to do.

Jesus lived on Earth with the purpose of fulfilling His assignment, and upon its completion, He returned to the Father in heaven and sits at the right hand of the Father, symbolizing a finished task. His life exemplified the concept of being born full and dying empty, as He selflessly gave everything He had to humanity. On the cross, as Jesus died, He cried out, "It is finished." His actions and teachings are well-documented in the Bible, providing us with real accounts of the multitude of remarkable things He accomplished.

It is also mentioned by John, one of the disciples of Jesus, that there were many other things that Jesus did which remain unknown to us. If these actions were to be recorded in detail,

John supposes that even the entire world would not be able to contain the books that would be written, giving an exact account of the works and words of the Lord Jesus. Truly, this is an astounding thought.

This leads us to reflect on our own achievements during our earthly existence. Considering that Jesus accomplished a great deal in just three years of his ministerial assignment, we must pause and ask ourselves: What have we achieved in the past three years that can be attributed to our presence in the universal shop of life, with the abundant gifts and talents bestowed upon us? Have we captivated people's attention enough for them to be drawn into our shop? Have they been transformed upon entering, making purchases, or have they left empty- handed, dissatisfied, and disappointed? Has our universal shop made a significant impact on the grandest avenue of life?

The time will eventually come when we must all return to our Creator. It could occur at any age. However, what truly matters most is that we have fulfilled our purpose on Earth. The words of Jesus, emphasizing the completion of the work He was sent to do, often echo in my mind. Since I discovered this scripture, it has become a powerful force in my life. It keeps me focused on fulfilling my earthly assignment and enables me to someday proudly declare that I have glorified God throughout my life on Earth.

Once again, I turned my attention to Revelation 20:12, where it states, "And I saw the dead, great and small, standing before the throne, and books were opened. Another book was opened, which is the book of life. The dead were judged according to what they had done as recorded in the books." It is important to note that John the apostle of Jesus witnessed not only the dead, but individuals of all statuses—both great and small. Moreover, he saw not just one book, but multiple books. This signifies that regardless of our age, a record of our earthly lives exists.

All individuals, regardless of their status, will stand before God as the books are opened. It is also noteworthy that the books were opened, not just the book of life. The book of life represents our qualification for entry into heaven by accepting Jesus Christ as our saviour.

But there are other books as well. These books bear our names inscribed on them, containing a record of everything we did on Earth, whether good or bad. Jeremiah 29:11 declares, "'For I know the plans I have for you,' says the LORD, 'plans to prosper you and not to harm you, plans to give you hope and a future.'" Within those other books lie all the thoughts and plans that God intends for us to fulfil on Earth, encompassing the thoughts He has of us, the dreams He has placed within us, the people we were meant to bless, the souls we should have brought to the salvation of the Lord Jesus, and the talents and gifts we possess, whether utilized or not all meticulously documented.

Our entire lives are recorded in those other books, and it is from them that both the great and the small will be judged based on their actions on the Earth. May God continually teach us to value each day as we strive to complete the race set before us and fight the good fight of faith until we return to our Creator. On that day, when we are no longer present in our physical bodies but dwell in the presence of the Lord, we shall be alive and well.

If one passes away without fulfilling their life's mission and calling, the plane of destiny sadly departs with an empty seat, as they never showed up to claim their place for the journey. Whether travelling in first class or economy, the ultimate destination remains the same, and every passenger disembarks at the same place, depending on whether it's a direct flight. If the flight includes multiple stops, some will depart while others will board and occupy the newly available seats.

In the race of life, we may begin the journey with certain people, but along the way, some may not reach the finish line and pass away, while others will be born. For some, the journey will be short, and they will disembark before others, whereas for others, the flight will be long.

The key is to finish well and finish strong, regardless of the duration of your race. I reiterate what the Bible teaches: "The race is not always won by the swift, the battle is not always won by the strong, and success does not always come to the wise or wealth to the brilliant. Time and chance happen to them all." We all have one chance at life, so it is essential to give it our best shot and strive for victory.

Remember, we only have one opportunity to perform on the stage of life before the final curtain closes and the earthly applause fades away.

CHAPTER 22

WHAT IS YOUR PURPOSE?

Why am I alive? "What is the purpose of all this? What am I here for?" These are profound questions that have been pondered by many individuals in their quests for the true meaning of life. As I explore this journey called life, I am beginning to understand that the essence of one's existence lies in discovering one's unique purpose. What does purpose mean, you might ask? It is simply understanding why you were created and uncovering your specific assignment or mandate in this world by fully maximizing your gifts, talents and calling.

You are here on Earth for a divine assignment. Your mission is to fulfil the plan and purpose that God has specifically designed for you, rather than solely pursuing your own desires. You may still be wondering what this purpose is. Well, the purpose of life is to operate as a valuable and necessary human being, rather than a constantly dependent one. You were created to love and serve God and others.

In a healthy human relationship, there must be a genuine willingness to prioritize serving the other person. When a relationship becomes self-centered and solely focused on fulfilling one's own interests, it becomes narcissistic in nature.

Indeed, our relationship with God can sometimes resemble that of a child's constantly asking their father for various things like blessings, protection, guidance, and love. However, it is also important to approach God without any specific requests and simply express our desire to connect with Him. We can come before God and say, "God, I really miss conversing with You today. I'm not asking for anything, but I just want to express my love and gratitude for how You care for me, guide me, protect me, and provide for all my needs." Imagine the joy our Heavenly Father would feel knowing that we love and appreciate Him simply for being there for us.

There are many aspects of life that remain mysterious and beyond our comprehension. That is a natural part of our human experience. Although I may not fully appreciate or comprehend the need for the things I do, I still carry them out.

For example, why is it necessary to consume three to four meals a day? I suppose it is for strength and to gain nutritional benefits. It appears that God has designed the human body to require sustenance. Similarly, I often question the need for six to eight hours of sleep each night. Is it for rest or energy, or maybe to remove toxins in the brain that build up while I'm awake? Perhaps I may never fully understand, but I believe it is all a part of God's magnificent design of the human body.

In the grand scheme of things, I did not request to be born or to die, nor did I ask for this life. Nevertheless, everything that God has designed serves a specific purpose, including you. Therefore, when I wake up each morning, perhaps the question I should ask is, "What does God require of me?" After all, He is the Creator who knows why I am here.

God did not make a mistake when He created me because my life was and is not wrong for me, and I am not a mistake. Similarly, your life is God's gift to you, so live it because it is yours and not anyone else's. It is your responsibility to take care of the temple of God: yourself.

Are you fulfilling your God-given purpose and plan for the life you have? Do you understand your individual assignment? What are you good at? What are you passionate about? What contribution does your existence on Earth make to the lives of others? Your answers to these questions define your purpose and validate your presence on Earth.

Understanding the distinct purpose for your existence and your aspirations will provide valuable perspective on your life's journey. As you reflect upon your life's conclusion, what kind of life do you desire to live? What legacy do you wish to leave behind?

It is important to acknowledge that there is a reason why you woke up this morning while others did not. This signifies that your work on this Earth is not yet complete. You have been granted another opportunity to serve God and make a difference in the lives of others. Embrace this privilege and use it to serve both God and your fellow human beings.

You are alive because there is something that only you can do, something for which no one else is equipped or gifted for. You possess a unique ability to accomplish your assignment and fulfil God's agenda on Earth.

Your existence matters and has purpose because God desires you to partner with Him, using your life to bless others rather than solely focusing on yourself. He deliberately chose you and knows your individual calling in life, enabling you to run your race with a clear objective.

Make certain that when you depart from this world, you leave having emptied out your resources by enriching others with everything you were given to share. Leave a lasting imprint so that your presence is felt and remembered.

Strive to fulfil your purpose and create a tangible record of a life well-lived. Let your name be etched in the hearts of those you encounter, leaving an indelible mark that withstands the test of time.

May the whole world yearn for an audience with you, eager to hear the wisdom and guidance that God has placed within your heart for those in need. Be a beacon of hope, a solution to the problems people face, and a key that unlocks the answers they seek.

CHAPTER 23

WHAT TRULY MATTERS MOST?

There is a story about a teacher who placed a huge empty jar in the front of a classroom. He then brought out a large pile of stones which he carefully began to fit into the jar one by one until he could fit no more stones. The teacher turned to the children and asked if the jar were full. The class answered with a resounding yes.

Then, from under the table, the teacher pulled out a large bag of small pebbles which he started pouring into the jar while shaking it slightly. The pebbles, being smaller in size, were able to fill up the open spaces among the stones. Again, he asked the youths if the jar were full. Some of the children answered confidently with another "Yes, it is now full." Others, however, were hesitant to answer while they watched carefully to observe the purpose of the demonstration. The teacher then pulled out a bag of sand and started pouring it into the jar. The children observed carefully as the tiny grains filled up all the remaining interstitial spaces among the stones. For the third time, he asked the class if the jar was full. This time a few of the children were still hesitant and answered, "Probably not."

Lastly, the teacher took a jug of water and poured it into the jar, saturating the sand and immersing the stones and pebbles. Gazing at the jar, the children realised that it was indeed full.

Catching the children's attention, the teacher said "I want you to realize that this jar is symbolic of your life. The stones signify the important things such as your family, your physical and mental health and well-being, and friends. These are the priceless things that matter most and will remain when all else has vanished. The pebbles are the other things that matter. Your house, your job, your business, your car. Additionally, the sand represents the small and trivial things in life that easily steal your joy and peace."

The teacher continued, "If you put the sand or the pebbles into your jar first, there will be no room for the stones. The same equates to life. If you occupy your time and energy with trivial things and mundane tasks, you will never have room for the things that truly matter the most. The stones signify the things critical to the true essence of our existence. The stones also represent quality time spent with loved ones, taking care of one's health, pursuing your dreams and passions.

"If you don't prioritize the primary things, you may find at the end of life that you have left out the most important things—the things that matter most." The teacher then admonished the class by saying, "Make sure you build a firm foundation that is secure by putting the stones into your jar first as your main pillars. These are your family, spouse, health, passions, and dreams. When everything else is stripped away, these will remain. Take care of the precious stones first because they are valuable. Make time for those you love.

"The sand and the pebbles are the secondary tasks that should not consume all your time and energy. Don't allow them to take precedence over the stones. At the end of your life's journey, it is the stones that will weigh the most in your jar of life. The stones will define the quality of a life well lived.

"Let your life be driven by the things that enrich your spirit, that fulfil your soul and invigorate your body—the things that matter the most. The rest are just pebbles and sand."

As the teacher concluded, a curious young girl asked what the water symbolized. The teacher replied, "The water signifies what holds relationships together. No matter how full your life may be, there is always time and room to meet with a friend for a drink. Regardless of how busy you are, there will always be opportunities to connect with people. The precious moments for relaxation, spontaneous laughter, connection with loved ones, and shared moments of joy. These are all critical to bonding."

In our lives we often find ourselves juggling so much in a single moment and trying to fit everything into one day. We get so caught up in the temporal and mundane tasks of doing things, that we forget what it means to experience life in the moment and have joy by doing what truly matters the most.

CHAPTER 24

'DO IT NOW'

Don't be the loudest mourner when you were the most silent lover in my life. Love me now.

Don't wait to remember me when you can no longer see me, and I am gone. Remember me now.

Don't forget my love for you but carry it in your heart as a token of God's everlasting love from me to you. Don't profess your love for me when I am gone and unable to reciprocate. Profess it now.

Don't postpone visiting my house when you can, because there will be a day when you won't find me at home. Visit me now.

Don't be eager to carry my casket in death when in life you never carried my burdens. Lift me now.

Don't sing love songs for me when I am dead and cannot hear them or am unable to appreciate their beautiful sound. Sing them to me now.

Don't bring me beautiful roses and place them on my grave, when I can no longer smell their fragrance. Bring the flowers now.

Don't frown upon my smile, for one day you may miss it when the mere mention of my name brings sadness. I won't be present to witness your smile. Smile at me now.

Don't shed tears for me when I am gone if you didn't shed them with me during life's ups and downs. Let us cry together now.

Don't speak an abundance of kind words to my coffin when my lifeless body can no longer hear or appreciate them. Speak now, while I can still hear you.

Don't loudly praise me in death when you never celebrated me in life. Celebrate me now.

Don't express sorrow for my absence if you never shared in my present suffering. Share my suffering now.

Don't come to me in the evening when I am no longer here if you never showed up in the morning. Show up now.

Don't contribute money for funeral expenses when you refused to lend a helping hand during my trials. Give it to me now.

Don't decide to fly across oceans to see my lifeless form when you could not spare a moment to call and inquire about my well-being while I was living. Call me now.

Don't wait to be forgiven if you hurt me; I may not be around long enough to hear you say, 'I am sorry'. Apologize now.

Don't wait until it's too late to say, 'I love you'. Say it now when I can still hear you.

Whatever you must do, do it now, for tomorrow is not guaranteed to anyone.

CHAPTER 25

HOW I WANT TO BE REMEMBERED

As I recently read the biography of Dr. Sam Sasser (July 31, 1937 - September 27, 1995), a scholar, teacher, evangelist, author, and pastor, I was deeply moved by the notion that every life holds significance, and that each individual has the potential to make a profound impact, particularly when they discover their unique gifts, goals, and purpose.

It has dawned on me that it is possible to touch numerous lives without ever physically encountering every person. While I may not have had the privilege of meeting this extraordinary man, I am able to connect with him through his writings, even though he is no longer physically with us.

This realization prompts me to reflect upon who will have the opportunity to read my own story and whether I will be able to fulfil my destiny in a way that leaves a meaningful impact on my generation.

I was truly amazed while reading the autobiography of Dr. Sam Sasser, a man who was deeply cherished by thousands of Pacific Islanders. It is astounding to learn that he was responsible for founding 26 churches and dedicated his life as a missionary in the Marshall Islands and Samoa. Furthermore, he served as a pastor in Honolulu, California, and Texas, and actively participated in teaching at conferences and crusades in 63 different nations.

Such a remarkable individual, he had expressed his wish for his heart to be laid to rest in the Marshall Islands. During his Homegoing Celebration, the following prayer was offered in honour of Sam:

Now that I have gone to God,
I ask that you remember these things.
Bury my body, but do not bury my love.
Bury my eyes, but not my vision.
Bury my feet, but not the path of my life.
Bury my hands, but do not bury my efforts.
Bury my shoulders, but not the concern
I carried.
Bury my voice, but not my message.
Buy my mind, but not bury my dreams.
Bury me, but do not bury my life.
If you must bury something.
Bury my sins, my weaknesses.
But let my love for each of you continue.
In Jesus, Amen.

Dr. Sasser's words have made a profound impact on my heart, and I carry them with me constantly. It is humbling to realize that despite his untimely passing, he accomplished so much in such a short time, which fills me with a sense of wonder and great admiration without seeking to compare myself to him.

As mentioned earlier, when Jesus Christ was nearing the completion of His earthly mission, He declared, "I have glorified God on the Earth; I have finished the work that He [God] has given Me to do." Jesus finished young, but the impact of His life's work on the Earth is an account that will never cease to be told from generation to generation.

Service is the final stage where God uses your pain to heal others. God transforms your pain into your life's message, enabling you to serve Him and minister to others who are going through similar experiences. It is written that we should comfort others with the comfort that we have received from God. Your ministry emerges from your own pain.

When I depart from my earthly existence, I aspire to echo the words of Jesus Christ as my parting message to loved ones and all who have encountered the story of my life. My desire is to finish well and finish strong. The knowledge that I have faithfully run my race and fulfilled my earthly purpose through service will bring me the greatest joy and fulfilment when I stand before my Creator in that final hour, to give an account of my life on Earth.

Regardless of the challenges and hardships that life presents, and no matter how intensely life's trials may strike, I encourage you never to surrender the fight for your existence. The battle is not over until the final whistle blows, signalling the end of your struggle. And lastly, when your time to depart draws near and the final act concludes on the stage of life, ensure that you live out your life's purpose and leave no task unfinished.

Make the most of your time on Earth and strive to leave behind evidence of your existence. Leave a profound impact so that others may see your footprints in the sand and recognize that you walked upon this Earth.

May your name resonate through the annals of history, echoing from generation to generation.

CHAPTER 26

TRACE ME

My deepest desire is not only for the remembrance of my life's story, but more importantly, for the resounding recognition of the great God I serve and represent on Earth. May it be known that He was my strength and anchor every time I stumbled. As my journey unfolds through my writings, I long to be remembered as someone who passionately loved God and humanity. I do not wish to depart from this Earth without leaving a lasting impact.

Trace my existence through my books, trace it through my endeavours, trace it through my songs, trace it through my children, and trace it through the ministry I have established to bring hope and healing to the broken-hearted.

Trace my footsteps through my devoted husband of many years, trace them through the love shared with my family and friends, and trace them through the influence of my mother. Yes, trace me through my genuine care and compassion for others, and you will discover my essence.

It is my utmost desire not to be remembered as a distant memory of a self-centered life, vanishing without leaving a mark.

My presence on this Earth must create a difference that reveals that I was born with, and for a purpose. I must provide solutions and bring positive transformation to the lives of the many individuals I encounter. May the lives of people be forever changed upon encountering me, as I carry a presence that impacts their very being.

I find great wonder in the account of King Solomon, known as the wisest and richest man to have ever lived, as depicted in the Bible. It is said that people from all corners of the world sought his audience, travelling great distances to be in his presence, seeking his counsel and listening to the wisdom bestowed upon him by God.

This account leads me to reflect on the impact I am making in the lives of those who encounter me. I hope and pray that many will also seek an audience with me, desiring to benefit from the wisdom and guidance I may be able to offer, just as they did with King Solomon.

The essence of every individual, from the moment they are born until their last breath, carries a fragrance that leaves a distinct and unique aroma associated with their being.

I am reminded of a former acquaintance who remarked that they possessed the ability to discern my presence despite my physical absence, stating that there remained a subtle fragrance unmistakably signalling my presence lingering in the surrounding atmosphere, which revealed undeniable evidence of my visitation.

It is imperative never to contemplate ending one's life, for such a decision would be a grave mistake when faced with the presence of the Creator. Instead, endeavour to embark on a journey of self-discovery, unravelling the depths of who you are and what you were destined to be and accomplish.

Never depart from this Earth without fully understanding what your purpose is and wholeheartedly embracing it.

When the time comes for me to depart from this earthly realm, having fulfilled my assignment, I desire my name to resonate and be traceable wherever it is spoken or mentioned.

I urge you not to disappear from this world without leaving a trace. May the future generations be able to find you in the archives of famous libraries, in the memories and hearts of the people you have touched throughout your life's journey.

May people remember your smile, your embrace, your fragrance, your kiss, your words, your comforting presence, your unwavering support, your faith, your joy, your peace, your resilience, your courage, your encouragement, your inner and outer beauty, your purity, and most importantly, your love for humanity and for God.

Rid yourself of all negativities that drive people away. Choose to embrace life and the people around you, including those whom you have yet to meet. Be traceable.

CHAPTER 27

HEART TO HEART

This book is based on my personal journey as I navigate through the depths of grief, love, loss, healing, joy, and the pursuit of hope amidst profound despair. It stands as my most challenging endeavour yet, as I intimately relive the experiences that have shaped me. The act of writing about my personal trials and triumphs has become a transformative and healing odyssey, enabling me to weave real-life events into a compelling narrative.

My aspiration is for this memoir to resonate deeply within the hearts of its readers while also leaving an indelible mark on recorded history—a testament to my family, friends, and the entire world.

I owe my ability to overcome life's numerous trials and challenges to the unwavering love of my beloved Jesus Christ, God the Father, and God the Holy Spirit. Simply put, God in

Three persons—Blessed Trinity, including the support and care from my loved ones. It is through God's boundless love that I have discovered a profound sense of hope, peace, and joy that cannot be found elsewhere.

I cherish the gift of life, which I have come to call 'Amazing Grace,' and through it, I have personally experienced and embraced the promise of God's enduring presence in my life.

I would never have been able to write an account of my life's griefs and joys had it not been for the challenges that I faced.

These challenges, which the devil used to deter me from my assignment, inflicted wounds meant to break and crush me. However, God worked everything out for my good. He helped me discover the strength, courage, and resilience that are born out of suffering and pain.

Additionally, loss, grief, pain, joy, and anguish have taught me that life is an immeasurable gift to be cherished daily. Therefore, life must be lived in the moment, fully embraced, and equally enjoyed.

Sometimes we may ask the question, "Does Jesus care when my heart is wounded?" When the pain becomes too deep, heavy, and indescribable, and the burdens weigh heavily on our weary souls, and the path ahead grows dark, lonely, and dreary. Yet, His response echoes, "Yes, I care." When death inevitably comes to claim our loved ones, leaving our hearts saddened, lonesome, and dejected, their absence creates an irreplaceable void in our lives and families.

The realization that in every trial, there was always sufficient grace to carry me through, even when my path was unclear and I could not feel God's presence, brings great consolation. He was there all along, silently watching, steadfastly holding my hand, and continuously wiping away my tears. His constant assurance that He will never abandon or forsake me, regardless of the intensity of the storm, gives me strength.

I hope that my story serves as a teaching and a reminder about the complexities of life. Life, with all its beauty and richness, also carries its share of challenges and hardships. Just like a rose, which exudes a lovely fragrance but is adorned with sharp thorns, life presents us with its twists and turns, revealing its less pleasant aspects even when we are unprepared for unfortunate circumstances.

This serves to remind us that on this earthly journey, we are mere wandering pilgrims, often navigating through dimly lit paths. Therefore, we should strive to live our lives to the fullest with the resources available to us.

The words from the Bible remind us that when mankind had become corrupted in the period preceding the flood, God said: "My Spirit shall not abide in man forever, for he is flesh; his days shall be a hundred and twenty years" (Genesis 6:3).

Furthermore, another Bible interpretation states that the days of our life are seventy years, or even by reason of strength are eighty years, yet their span is but toil and trouble; they are soon gone, and we fly away.

For we are like vapour that appears for a little while, then vanishes. So, may God teach us to number our days, that we may gain a heart of wisdom.

As we reach the end of our life's journey, it is my belief that we will not approach our Saviour empty- handed, but rather offer a trophy as a testament to our experiences and growth.

Human beings should not depart from this world carrying all the gifts and potential that were bestowed upon them at birth; instead, they should leave behind a legacy by utilizing and sharing those gifts to make a positive impact on Earth.

So, regarding your own life, I ask you this question: What will you be remembered for?

BIBLIOGRAPHY

Dr Sam Sasser (July 31, 1937 - September 27, 1995). Pacific Mission Outreach. https://pacmiss. org › Sam Sasser

English Standard Version Bible (ESV)

New King James Bible (NKJV)

New International Version Bible (NIV)

Schneider Philipp T (2016), Balanced Action. https://balancedaction. me/2012/10/17/the-jar- of- life-first-things-first

The Colonel's Story Timeline | The Life of Harland Sanders 9 September 1890 - December 16th, 1980. https://en.wikipedia.org › wiki › Colonel Sanders

www.ingramcontent.com/pod-product-compliance
Lightning Source LLC
Chambersburg PA
CBHW061733050726
47598CB00002B/463